A Journey To Motherhood

By Devin Hammon

Introduction

My name is Devin Hammon and I deal with
infertility on a daily basis.

This book contains my ups and downs, heartbreaks
and disappointments. The bottom line is this: I am not
defined by my infertility. I decided long ago I would
not let it beat me or my dream of having a family.
Today I look back and am amazed at the way God
used my struggle to heal and grow not just myself but
also those around me.

I have learned to love every part of this journey. I have

learned that it is okay to not be okay with the heartache of the past and the betrayal of my body. I've learned to live broken and am discovering how to love myself in my very own brokenness. Through the brokenness I gained a family in a very unconventional way.

I've never been someone who does well keeping silent. I like to describe myself as an open book, so maybe it's a little ironic I'm sharing a book with you now. It is sure to give you way more information then you ever wanted to know about a complete stranger. I want to stress that this is a record of **MY** journey. I have a story to tell, yet my intention is not to impose my feelings or beliefs upon my readers. If my experience or perspective helps even one person in their journey then this book will have been worth my time and effort. You may be going through this same thing, day after day, heartbreak after heartbreak, yet you push on. Know this – if you have ever experienced the struggle that comes with infertility, loss, stillbirth or even adoption – you are a warrior!

Trigger Warning: I will be discussing in depth and very great detail some very hard emotional and physical stories from my life. This can be difficult for some to read and process. I will place a "Trigger Warning" before these sections that I feel may be hard for some to read.

Chapter One

Everyone seems to have an idea of how his or her future family life will look. Maybe we imagine a big house with a yard or a studio apartment in a big city with a family of cats or dogs keeping us company. No matter what it is, we get an idea in our head of how the average family looks. We meet people who are different from us and think, "Wow, I could never do that." Sometimes we admire these people and wish that we were more like them; other times we sit back and think of all the ways we are better than them.

If my personal journey of becoming a mother, growing my family, and loving people the way I do now was laid out before me ten years ago, I would have laughed at the idea. You see I was (okay, okay— still am) someone who likes to have my life planned out to a T. Of course, nothing ever turns out how we want it to 100% (maybe not even 20%), but that is not necessarily a bad thing. We have to learn to embrace ourselves in our journey right where we are. As life moves forward we are forced to either fight against the current or sit back and let it lead us on our very own journey. This journey has taught me to sit back and let go.

Where would I say my journey to motherhood began? I suppose I would say it began as a little girl. I grew up pretending to be a mommy to little families of plastic dolls or stuffed animals. I cooked, cleaned, and changed diapers all wrapped up in imaginary bliss. As I grew up my mind began to switch from playing mom to thinking, "Oh, I'm not ready for that yet." After marriage—when pregnancy became a real possibility—the mere idea of it petrified me. We were not ready. But as time went on that little niggling desire to mother stirred once again. Eventually we decided it was time to start a family, and I naively believed it would be easy. I saw all these families around me and knew that it was going to be me within a year. But when month-after-month went by without success, that single negative line seemed to give us the finger every time. Eventually, I began to accept that something was wrong. Every day became a guessing game. I analyzed every single thing that came out of my body. Every twinge or cramp became a possible pregnancy symptom. For five years the battle to overcome infertility became my life.

What did infertility look like for me? Infertility meant avoiding eye contact with visibly pregnant women. It meant pretending I was busy when I walked through the baby isle at the store. Infertility meant pretending I didn't see children—even when I was around them. I stopped holding my friend's baby when everyone was taking a turn. This wasn't because I was annoyed or didn't like children. Rather, when I looked at them my pain felt unbearable. My own body reminded me what I did not have on a daily basis, so seeing a child's laughing, smiling, beautiful face just seemed to tear that hole in me even bigger. Infertility is a daily battle that occupies every thought, every waking moment. I could get busy to feel accomplished, positive, and happy, but at the end of the day I still felt that horrible emptiness.

When I wrote the above description, I was at the two-year mark of actively trying to start a family and on the third month of seeking fertility help from a specialist. There were times when I was mopey and frustrated. Yet, I was determined to beat it. I wasn't going to let my body tell me what I could and could not have. I wasn't willing to give up. One way or another I was going to be a mother to a home full of children.

Chapter Two

I began to travel from the moment I was old enough to sign up for church mission trips. I didn't care where they were going; I just wanted to go. By age seventeen I had been to Mexico, Jamaica, Panama, and Romania. My first trip to Romania took place in the summer of 2004. I had just finished my junior year of high school and saved enough money for a two-month summer mission trip. The organization I traveled with took teenagers all over the world to different countries for different purposes.

It was on this trip to Romania that I met my future husband. He actually signed up with the same organization to go to Kenya, but due to the civil unrest they made the wise choice to cancel that trip. He was offered the opportunity to come join my team in Romania instead. It was not love at first sight or anything close to it. I did in fact fall in love that summer, but it was with the country and people of Romania. I could feel God tugging my heart and almost audibly calling my name. I just knew that my life was going to change forever and that I had to come back. It wasn't just a desire; it was so much more. Every fiber of my being knew I was meant to go back to Romania for a year. If I didn't go back, I wouldn't be where I was supposed to be, and I would be haunted every day with that thought.

In order to make this dream happen and to be able to support myself financially for that year I worked as much as I possibly could as I finished my senior year of high school. Every bit of free time I had was filled with fundraisers such as spaghetti dinners, car washes and even support letters to help raise enough money for a year's income. I saved every penny I could so that I could move back to Romania as soon as I graduated high school. In the summer of 2005 –just one month after high school graduation –I did just that. With a meager budget between $400-$500 a month, I moved oversees, and my life changed forever. I rented an apartment with two other girls who I had met on my trip the year before who felt the same tug I had. It was a relief to not only have a built in support system but to also have others who spoke fluent English.

By the time I left Romania I was pretty fluid with the Romanian language, but I definitely wouldn't call myself fluent. My year in Romania was a beginning for so many things in my life. It was a time when healing from my past occurred and confidence for my future grew. It was a time when God began to stir the passions in me that where there from the beginning; I just hadn't known how strongly.

While in Romania, my passion for helping others just exploded! I was able to find two places to volunteer my time. One I connected to through my roommates, but it was only part-time. I volunteered at the Children's Hospital in a ward for abandoned babies. Yes, you heard me correctly –abandoned babies. Believe it or not infant abandonment still happens in many countries. The general idea of this job was to provide the stimulation the infants needed by cuddling and loving them. Have you ever heard of "failure to thrive"? It is when infants and children are left alone without necessary stimulation, human contact and a nurturing environment which in turn causes them to not form healthy attachments and not to develop into healthy, functioning human beings. These children would lie in a crib all day long without any stimulation. If it were not for the volunteers that would love on these kids, most would have had no human contact apart from the nurses doing their rounds.

My second and main full time job was at Casa

de Lumina (House of Light). This wonderful home worked as both a shelter for women (many of whom were exiting the sex industry and trying to find a new way to support themselves) and as a Romani kindergarten. Romani children were not welcomed in Romanian schools at this time. Despite being born in Romania, other Romanians used their backgrounds against them to create a sort of caste system.

As I spent my time with these organizations, I discovered my true love for children and at eighteen years old I found my calling. I had no doubt that I wanted to foster, adopt, and be a mom to a house full of children.

During my year in Romania I made friends with a particular gang of homeless street children (yes, you read that correctly). Many children run away from orphanages or bad home situations and create their own family gangs. They live in subway systems, the park, and the street; they are homeless. Let that sink in for a minute. The problem is that it is normal; it is normal in many countries. As I formed relationships with these kids by bringing them food, talking with them, and providing clothing when I could, I was designated to their "do-not-touch" list. I was exempt from picked pockets, stealing, and other survival tactics. I got to know one particular eight- or nine-year-old young man quite well. I swear that sometimes he seemed to follow me around the city. Seeing each other resulted in huge hugs and then holding hands as we walked throughout the city. He craved a protective, mothering touch. He would ask if I wanted to hear him sing; as we walked he would sing for me. This young boy was a child, yet he had no home to call his own. Living on the street was better than living in the orphanage he had run away from. At least on the street no one would beat him; he could control his destiny. So many times I found him huffing from a bag of glue in his hands. He did this not just to feel high, but to help curb the hunger and physical pains from extra hard days or weeks. It helped numb the coldness of winter nights. Now, I didn't speak fluent enough Romanian to get this gang's entire story, but how I wish I could have! I wish I had been able to tell each of them how very special they were and how they were worth more than this society had led them to believe. Though I couldn't tell them these things, I learned to tangibly love them through their hurts, aches, and pains. They taught me so much, and perhaps my biggest lesson as an eighteen-year-old was that I had a desire to protect these kids and love them as my own.

There was a particular abandoned infant named Gabriel who I bonded with at the Children's Hospital. If you could have seen him, you would have seen how much he looked like me; almost as if he could have been my child. Maybe that was why I felt so drawn to him. I made it a personal mission to do all I could to make sure that he thrived on my days there, and my heart became so very attached. I wanted to adopt him. I wanted to stay in Romania, get my residency, and care for this beautiful baby boy. I remember tearfully calling my mom and telling her I wanted to do this. Barriers be damned—this young baby needed someone to love him when I was gone, and I needed to make sure he had that person. Full of tears and heartache, I told my Mom I wanted to stay in Romania and adopt him. As only a mom could, she lovingly pointed out that this was an emotional – not a thought out or even spiritual – decision. I was eighteen. I had enough money for only one year with no other expected income. In order to get Romanian residency, I would have had to live there for five years.

During this hard but necessary conversation, something else happened in my heart. My desire to adopt solidified; I knew it would never go away. I now knew how deeply I would be able to love a child that wasn't my own. The idea of fostering and adopting became more than a thought – it became a true desire. I thought of the street children and those older kids who had already lost so much needed love.

They needed someone to fight for them when they couldn't fight for themselves. I knew that one day, I was going to be that person.

Chapter Three

During my time in Romania Isaac and I became really close. I was from Louisiana and he was from Pennsylvania, so it was funny to me how God began to bring us together when we went from half a country to half a world apart. Throughout my senior year we talked occasionally and caught up via the typical "what's new" scenario. As my time drew closer to Romania we began to get closer; once I was in there the relationship began to grow even more. They say communication is the key in any relationship, I can tell you we found this to be true—

we had no lack of communication. Sending him email updates turned into weekly phone calls; I began to fall in love with him through the distance. I opened my heart, sharing the emotions and hardships of my day. I began to call him constantly – for some unexplained reason I felt a real connection. He talked me through things I had never felt before. Slowly but surely, we arrived to a point were we talked on the phone at least a couple times a week. To me, our friendship was becoming more than "just friends." This man I poured my heart out to began to open up as well, with that I saw a man who had similar passions, desires, and goals. I saw a man I thought I wanted to spend the rest of my life with. This was a new feeling for me! I had never had a boyfriend; I had never even been on a date (and no, it wasn't because I wasn't asked). Believe it or not, I had been told I was "the one" more than once by friendly guys. I just wasn't interested. I didn't feel the need to waste my time in a relationship with someone that I didn't see my future self with. Isaac changed that. I wanted to marry this guy who was halfway across the world. But how on earth would something like that even start? I mean, he was already my best friend. How could something go from friendship to more than friends without turning into a complete fiasco? I knew I wanted it, but I also knew there was no way it could happen while I was halfway across the world. I think this is partly what helped me say goodbye to my Romanian family (many of whom I still keep in contact with). They will always have a huge place in my heart, and I love each and every one of them. I do hope I can see them again.

When I moved back to Louisiana, life didn't click with me like I thought it would. People at home didn't treat me any differently, but that was actually part of the problem. My year in Romania forced me to grow into someone way older than nineteen. I had held dying children in my arms, and loved, taught and provided for orphans and prostitutes. I went from living with children who literally had no idea where their next meal was coming from to waiting tables in a restaurant listening to people complaining that the meal they received was sub-par. I felt as if everyone expected me to fall right back into who I was before I left, but that person was gone forever. During my year in Romania, I had learned the stories of those who were battered and broken and learned to love them and help them find a way to put themselves back together.

Arriving back home felt like losing a huge part of my identity. In the middle of this seemingly limbo stage, I was able to form two new friendships within my local Church, and they were instrumental in helping me feel grounded. They helped me continue to grow and reach past first-world problems into local places where I felt I could pursue the calling on my life and make a difference locally.

About a month after arriving back home, Isaac and I stepped into the beginning of a long (though shorter than before) distance relationship. The way we got there was actually pretty hilarious. For a while, Isaac would give me little hints via good ol' internet messaging that he might want something more in our relationship. I in turn would sometimes hint back, all while pulling out my Sherlock Holmes hat and monocle to try and decrypt what he had just said to me. As you can tell, I was already smitten and ready to give away my heart in a box with a pretty pink bow. There was one particular conversation where he straightforwardly asked if I felt like I had special feelings for anyone in particular. Taken aback by this very forward question, I immediately responded, "No," (and almost instantly regretted it). My mind was a cascade of thoughts ranging from: "Why did I not tell him yes?" to "What if he was trying to hint at something more?" I began to realize that our relationship was no longer healthy for me. I was constantly trying to read between the lines to find deeper meanings. So, I decided to take the plunge, put on a brave face, and boldly face my dilemma head on. If he didn't have feelings for me, then the way I felt about him needed to change. My feelings about our relationship would need to dwindle and die, and that wasn't going to happen with me talking to him multiple times a day. I sent him a text and asked if he could call me when he got the chance. Almost immediately my phone rang; it was him. I ran outside to my car in order to talk privately and let it all out. My one-sided conversation went something along these lines: "Listen, you asked me if I had feelings for anyone, and I told you no. That wasn't entirely truthful. I really REALLY like you. I want to be more than just friends, but if you don't feel this way I need you to tell me right now so that I can take a step back and get over you." Picture this all spoken with the speed of a roadrunner. I then began to ramble the same thing all over again when my speech was interrupted with, " Devin, Devin...." (I quieted myself.) "I was in the process of writing you the same question via email." And that my friends—as simple as it sounds—is how it all began.   After talking constantly for almost a year and knowing each other for two, we had become best friends. I was ready to move forward, and so was he. I wish I could tell you our relationship experienced happily ever after and that we had the most perfect dating relationship there ever was, but let's be realistic and admit that that never happens. It would also make this book very boring. As our relationship grew, I began to realize I no longer wanted to stay in Louisiana. I felt I had nothing holding me there. So as Isaac during the school year moved from his hometown of York, Pennsylvania (PA) to Pittsburgh, PA in order to attend college, I began to work to save money to move to Pennsylvania. I decided I would work for a year in Louisiana and then head to York, PA in order to get to know Isaac's family. I figured that because it was only a four-hour drive to Pittsburgh, we would still be able to see each other fairly often. However, what full time young adult or college student has eight hours to spend in the car on their only day off? During this year Isaac and I remained in different states, and only saw each other a handful of times. But we still talked every day all day long. I will say this: long distance relationships are hard. They require a ton of work, trust, and sacrifice. An old co-worker asked me how I could be in a relationship with a guy in another state, never knowing if he was being faithful when I wasn't there. I gave her the simplest but truest response I could think of, "Why would I be in a relationship with someone who I couldn't trust and needed to worry about his commitment?" She honestly did not know how to respond. Truthfully, I did have major moments of jealousy, including one absolutely crazy moment when I had a dream he kissed another girl and I called him to curse him out for something he never did. Yes—I did that. There was also tension and anger mostly due to miscommunication. Yet, we did it, and we are stronger because of it. We were forced to communicate and talk about our feelings because we couldn't see each other. We were forced to make time for each other and remind each other of how important we were in the other's life. Looking back, I have no regrets from dating long-distance. We made it three very long but very worth it years. In a way, I think it helped us get through the hardest year of our marriage—the first year.

Chapter Four

In June 2009 we finally bridged the gap; we were no longer were long-distance. Isaac graduated from a Pittsburgh college, so he thought he would see a lot of local work opportunities. He wanted to stay in Pittsburgh and felt that it would be pretty easy to find work in his field there. I packed up my apartment in York, PA, and we found a place to call our own in Pittsburgh. On June 21st, we were married.

I was so naive before we got married! We had never lived together at this point, and I thought that we would have amazingly sweet wedded bliss. Honestly, it's almost a miracle our relationship survived. I'm sure many of you who know me personally are sitting back right now nodding your heads saying, "I remember that." You see in 2008 we Americans were hit with what is now called *The Great Recession*. Our entire economy seemed to crash, and everyone I knew began to struggle. In 2009, we were still in the midst of this economic crisis.

Isaac was unable to find work not only in his field but in any type of job. He went to fast food and retail stores, personally talked to managers, and was told the same thing over and over again: "I'm sorry – you're just overqualified. We can't give you this position." We did have some income because I had (thankfully!) gotten a job as a waitress in a local restaurant, but to call it a steady income would have been a very big overstatement. We tried to get him a job at the restaurant where I worked, but Corporate said, "No." It seemed no one wanted to put in the time and effort of training someone if there was a risk of him leaving for a better job right after he was done training. I supported us for the first year of our marriage.

On top of this stress, I now had a constant companion. I loved Isaac dearly, with all my heart, but I never had any alone time at our house. I went from living on my own for years to boom—zero privacy ever. I was stressed beyond belief as the monthly bills came in, yet I had to keep going. I knew I couldn't stop. I was the one who was paying the bills. I was the one who was supporting us. Within a matter of months my savings account I had brought into our marriage was zeroed out. I knew I needed to do something that would help me make more money in the future. I took the plunge and went to cosmetology school to learn to do hair. This was something that I had been thinking about doing off and on for several years, but there were a couple reasons I decided that now was the time to do it. One was that money was so tight. Since my only job was at the restaurant, I had open availability to work any shift. Suddenly, management seemed to only be scheduling me for lunch shifts that no one else wanted, and we couldn't survive or pay our bills with those shifts. I thought that if I went to school during the day and changed my availability to work at night, management would schedule me in the evenings so I could make more money. I started attending school from 8:00AM-4:00PM Monday through Friday and working from

4:30PM-12:AM Tuesday through Saturday. I'm sure many of you readers can relate to a hectic schedule like this.

A few months after I started beauty school, Isaac managed to get a holiday position working fourteen hours a week at a nearby chain store. We were so happy to have any kind of extra income, but the only problem was that his shifts started at 2:00AM and bus lines weren't running at that time. Since we only had one car, I had to wake up, take him to work, drive back home for a few hours rest, and then get to school by 8:00AM. For months, other than on my Sundays off, I only got a few hours of uninterrupted sleep per twenty-four hour period. Yet, I still had to go full force at school and work. There was no other option.

After a couple of months of this, my body said, "Enough!" and began to shut down. I'm sure this was due to the lack of sleep, the high stress, and the amount of caffeine I was using just to keep myself moving. One night I woke up to consistent heart palpitations; but what was even scarier was I could feel my heart literally skipping beats. This scared me, so I rushed to an urgent care facility. They gave me a simple stress test in which I had to stand up, touch my toes, sit down, walk so many steps, etc. They were able to see that my heart was overworking by observing it on the EKG. They asked me my schedule and told me to stop, slow down, and allow myself rest. If I didn't, I could count on very serious issues in the future. I didn't know what to do! I needed to work to support us, and I needed to go to school – how was I going to take care of myself? I talked with my bosses and re-arranged my schedule so that I could have two days off in a row during the week. This would allow me to rest and recuperate. I also cut my hours back so that I would no longer be closing the restaurant every single day. This allowed me to leave closer to 10PM instead of 12AM most nights.

A week later, Isaac was called for an interview for a job in his field, and he almost immediately received the position. I felt as if a weight had literally been lifted off my shoulders. When he called to tell me the news, I was at school so I rushed outside thinking it was an emergency. As he gave me the news, I paced the sidewalk crying and praising God for His provision. We were going to make it. I have to stress to you all the reality of our situation in that last year. I really have no idea how we paid our bills.

As a server, I was paid cash at the end of my shifts,

and I would come home and put it all into an envelope.

When it came time to pay bills, somehow that

envelope was never empty even when it should have

been. We both feel like that was the first miracle we

witnessed together in our marriage (though there were

many more to come).

Chapter Five

As you can imagine, we weren't ready to be

parents after such a hard first year, so like many

couples we used contraception to prevent an

unexpected pregnancy. We felt we needed to be at a

more stable place before conceiving, and beyond that

we needed to get to know each other in a less stressful

time and figure out how to actually live together. I remember that a couple months into marriage I kept worrying about getting pregnant if our birth control failed. Had I known the difficult journey we would walk to start our family, I would have felt much differently. It is easy for me to get upset with myself for possibly preventing a miracle during that season, but the truth is this story that you are reading is my journey to motherhood, and it wouldn't have come about the way it had without these hardships and life lessons. My mistakes, regrets, and choices are all a part of it. I have learned the true miracle not only of conception and birth but also that every child is a gift more precious than gold.

About two years into our marriage (after a year of stable income from both Isaac and I), I felt as though I was ready to begin trying for a family. I wanted to be a mom and have a house full of children. We both knew the future had children for us; both adopted and biological. In fact, to this day we still debate about what a houseful of children actually means. I haven't quite won my loving husband over to my number yet but I think he is getting there. At that time, Isaac wasn't quite ready. We talked it out and decided to wait another year before starting down that road. Before we knew it, the year came and went and we revisited the situation. Isaac now felt that he was ready. He had a good job, and we had just bought our first house. It made sense that this would be our next step, and we thought it would be easy. Just two weeks after going off of my birth control pill, we went on a cruise and my naive little mind told me I shouldn't drink any alcohol because I was probably already pregnant. Seriously, you hear all these stories of people getting pregnant from one-night stands, and there are reality TV shows showing thirteen and fourteen year olds having babies. If they could do it, then we had this…how very deceived we were.

I spoke to a good friend about my frustrations after nine months or so passed with no pretty pink lines appearing on pregnancy tests. She recommended a book that would help me better learn my body and find the optimal time to get pregnant. I took her recommendation and learned so much about my body because of that book. I was able to be my own health advocate with that knowledge, because we all know that knowledge is power. Yet, while I was so grateful for this information, my crazy spiraling and obsession began. Every morning's routine included checking my temperature and recording every bodily fluid or discharge that came out of my body. We had to have sex every other day but not on certain days so that we could build up a "sperm army" and time intercourse for the exact days surrounding ovulation. Confusing isn't it? Not to many of you! In fact, many who have been through fertility treatments are sitting back nodding their heads and throwing their hands in the air shouting, "I feel you sister!" In sum, the act of making love and just being together became a task – one more chore to check off the list. Slowly, the joy was stripped away, though thankfully not all the time. This went on for a little over a year, and I began to realize as I charted my body month-to-month that my body wasn't doing what it was supposed to do. I realized I was not going to get pregnant on my own.

I kept Isaac constantly in the loop for all of this. In fact, I think he would have preferred to be a little less in the loop. No way! We were in this together, and my verbal processing mind was not letting him get off that easy (pun intended). We had a serious discussion about where to go from here. Adoption had always been a dream of ours, but was now really the right time for it? Should we dive right into that, or should we start smaller and see what our options would be with a fertility specialist? Though I wanted to adopt, I so very badly also wanted to experience the awesome miracle of pregnancy. I wanted to experience childbirth and breastfeeding. I wanted to adopt, yes, but I also overwhelmingly wanted more.

On February 7th, 2014, we sat down with a fertility specialist. I brought her all my charts and assessments and any bit of information I thought might jump start this process. She asked us a lot of questions and laid out our best options. If we decided to take this route, we would need several tests and a lot of monitoring, and our insurance would only cover a portion of it. We asked about timelines and were told we would receive six cycles of monitoring and fertility medication before they would jump into to any type of in vitro fertilization (IVF). It was there in that office that I entered a world I never thought I would need to be a part of. But, it was also through entering this world that I made lifelong friends, many of whom I still talk with everyday.

Chapter Six

One thing important thing I discovered on my infertility journey is that it wears you down in every way – emotionally, relational – really in every area. You have to deal with your self-induced guilt and disappointment while constantly being bombarded with innocent questions such as, "When are you going to start a family?" You have to put on a brave face when yet another friend announces their pregnancy. You have to fight for a sense of normalcy because you are daily reminded that your body isn't doing what it is supposedly made to do naturally. You feel like you are missing something. You want to be happy for friends and family announcing they are expecting, but it is hard. Jealousy rears its ugly head at any moment, even when your mind knows it isn't right.

As I went through fertility treatments, I felt like

a rat in a lab. I felt like I was being experimented on to cure a disease. It's hard to fully describe the process and the feelings that come with fertility treatment diagnostics. Most people have no idea what it actually entails; I sure didn't until the time came. Maybe some of you picture yourself on plush couches, enjoying deep pressure massages with boxes of chocolate while you swallow a simple pill and endure a non-invasive procedure. In reality – fertility treatments are the polar opposite of this. Try and imagine (if you will) being in a sterile room, naked from the waist down, legs up in stirrups, with a dildo the size of a baseball bat being jammed into your vagina. (No – this is not an exaggeration, or at least I certainly didn't feel like it was at the time.) Fertility specialists use this lovely dildo to view all your innards that no one should ever be able to see. They see everything from how many eggs you are producing to how many you may have left. Now imagine radioactive procedures with dye flowing through your body to let them see your tubes and uterus as they x-ray your innards to make sure that nothing is preventing a healthy pregnancy. Imagine waking up at 5:00 AM to get to the treatment center in time for your almost daily blood draw or invasive vaginal ultrasound to check your hormones or egg growth – all before you have to go to work.

While at work, I checked my phone every five minutes as I waited to hear from my doctor. I couldn't miss a phone call. If everything looked good, I needed to go back in the next day for a procedure, or I might need to give myself a shot in the stomach to speed up egg production. The call could tell us that its time to start humping each other like rabbits because that one egg is about to hatch. (Yes, I can hear some of you gasp at the way I would even put this in a book!) But the reality of being constantly exposed, explored, poked, and prodded is that I have lost my filter and my modesty. However, you picked up this book to read it, and you're welcome to put it down at any time (though I do hope you continue of course). Back to the matter at hand – timed UN-emotional sex. Sounds pleasant, doesn't it? If everything looked good, we were required to schedule sex at specific times on our calendar. In this season, infertility robbed me of the joy of love making. Now, add in mood-altering medications and the side effects that accompanied them. These were enough for people to believe I had suddenly turned into a doppelganger of Jekyll and

Hyde. I also gained so much weight due to the synthetic hormones I was putting into my body. I did all of this simply to try to get my body to do what it was supposed to do on its own. My emotions ranged through sheer rage, sadness, panic, and anxiety and seemed to run away together to form a cult that decided my sanity was the enemy. As you see – there were no plush couches, massages, or boxes of chocolates waiting for me. While going through this I distinctly remember taking a picture of said baseball bat dildo and sending it to Isaac with the caption, "That is about to be inside of me!" My loving husband then responded, "Mine is bigger." This sums up the dynamic of our relationship! Through it all Isaac would try to do anything he possibly could to ease my discomfort, whether through humor or distraction, and to this day I am so grateful for that.

Trigger Warning

During the first month of medication my body decided not to respond. At all. Not even a little bit. My doctor was "mystified" by my situation; she had never encountered anything like it. She increased my medications for the next month (ergo an extra dose of crazy), but it was successful. We had our first ever positive pregnancy test right on the day that marked the second year of trying to conceive. We were over the moon! I can't even tell you how many pregnancy tests I took just to convince myself it was real. I listened to the doctor's voice mail telling us, "Congratulations!" over and over again. We immediately told our family and friends – finally, we were here! We had been asked so many times when we were going to start a family that we had opened up and let them know our struggles. Why hold back our joy now? Everyone was so excited for us! But just a few days later, I began to bleed, and just like that our miracle was gone.

I think one of the hardest parts was trying to convince myself that I was okay. After only being pregnant for a few days, it didn't really count as a pregnancy. Right? I felt embarrassed to tell my friends and family of our loss. I also felt ashamed; as if I had done something wrong. Everyone was excited for us, but especially our family. I knew this would hurt them as well.

I want to expound on those last couple sentences before we move forward. Society in general places a huge stigma on not talking about your fertility struggles, miscarriages, and infant losses. It's as if there is an unspoken rule that we are not to burden others with something they seem to think we never really had. I say NO MORE! When you lose a child (in any way) the loss is deep and heavy. The pain never goes away; every due date imprints on your brain as a reminder of what you lost. We as a society need to rally around these beautiful souls, both dads and moms, who have lost a piece of their heart and don't know how to move forward.

After this miscarriage, my HCG (pregnancy) hormones dropped down to zero almost immediately. However, my estrogen level was still very high. Because of this, my doctor decided to put me on birth control. This would get my hormones under control and allow us to jump right back in at the end of the month. I was a ball of fury and annoyance that entire month. Here I was wanting to be pregnant so badly, yet I was on birth control. I decided I would use this month to do everything I could on my own to lower my estrogen levels. I went as extreme as I could using online advice ranging from cutting out all caffeine and processed sugar to using essential oil regimens and ingesting chia seeds up to my eyeballs. Bluntly put, I felt miserable and was miserable to be around. Upon the arrival of my birth control induced period we began my third month of fertility drugs. This was of course accompanied with many early morning "magic dildo" dates, blood draws, and all the poking and prodding I could ever want for the rest of my life. It was on this cycle that we conceived our son, and I could stop here to pretend everything was all roses and rainbows; we finally had our miracle baby! But the truth was something else entirely.

Have you ever wanted something so badly that when you finally get it, you are afraid it will be taken from you? I felt this so many times during this pregnancy, and it was due to this feeling that we decided to only let a select few friends and family know we had gotten pregnant. I had been bleeding as if my period had arrived from the moment they told me I was pregnant, but my HCG numbers continued to increase and pointed to a growing, healthy baby. Yet the *shame* of our previous loss plus the fear of "what if" was very real. After about a week, the bleeding finally stopped as HCG continued to rise. This was such a good sign! At five weeks, we went in for our first ultrasound to confirm the pregnancy was in utero (versus ectopic), and everything looked good; as far as they could tell there was only one baby. They wanted to schedule another appointment in two weeks to see if the baby had a heart beat, so we decided we would wait two more weeks before we told everyone. (Though let's be honest, we were bursting at the seams!) It seemed we finally might be able to tell people we were going to have a family and see it come to fruition.

Two weeks came and went, and we heard the heartbeat of our beautiful little man. The relief and joy that washed over us in that moment was beyond anything I can ever describe. There. He. Was. Our little baby! To say we left excited would be a gross understatement! Less then twenty-four hours later, I received a voicemail asking me to come back in; my doctor reviewed the heartbeat video and saw something they missed, they wanted a more thorough imaging to make sure everything was okay. I called the office back in a panic; what could this be?! They couldn't tell me because they couldn't tell themselves. I remember going into that second ultrasound with my heart in my throat; I just wanted to know that everything was okay! Waiting for my doctor to review those results felt like an eternity. I kept telling myself to be calm; God was in control. If he wanted this baby born, nothing was going to be able to take it away. Finally, the doctor called me and said all the images looked good and nothing seemed amiss. That answer wasn't good enough for me. I wanted details. What did they think it was? Were they sure everything was okay? How can something seem wrong then seem okay the next moment? They assured me that the images just taken proved everything was fine. They thought they had seen an unidentified shadow that didn't belong, but it seemed to have disappeared. The relief I felt was tangible enough to taste! Once again I cried, only this time it was tears of joy.

Chapter Seven

Trigger Warning

I remember it like it was yesterday. October 31st 2014. We were finally ready to share the news with our families. We decided we would surprise Isaac's parents via an impromptu road trip to their house for my father-in-law's birthday, bringing along a pair of baby overalls and a Happy Birthday sign. We had to opt for a less personal approach for my family since they were so far away. I took a video of the heartbeat and texted it to everyone with a caption stating "Baby Hammon - Coming in June!" I received the expected congratulations, but the conversation I had with my youngest brother, Nathan, is forever emblazoned on my mind.

Instead of jumping right into the conversation, I feel the need to give a little back story on Nathan and I's relationship. Nathan and I were very close. Despite our age gap, he somehow managed to become part of my circle of friends, even when I was in high school. I took him kayaking, to the movies, and out to dinner with my group of friends, many of whom were in college. (I've seemed to always have older friends.) I was Nathan's constant playmate, and he was my shadow. Despite our closeness, he fought a battle I felt I couldn't help him with; he suffered from depression throughout adolescence—maybe even before junior high. He would open up to me about the emptiness and despair that seemed to constantly surround him for weeks at a time. I remember my parents seeking help for him through therapy, medications, etc., but even then there were times when he was in such a dark place and couldn't seem to be reached. My parents would ask me to talk to him, and I remember a lot of conversations in his room, lit with the glow from his little fish tank, just talking or sitting together shoulder to shoulder on his bed in silence. He couldn't always articulate his words, and at the time I was so naive to what it truly meant to be depressed. He tried to tell me his feelings, but since he couldn't even pinpoint where they came from, the most I could do was love him through it. He would let me pray for him and talk to him about God and finding a purpose to keep going, but he would also tell me that I really didn't understand. And you know what? He was right. It hasn't been until recently that I have been able to truly understand depression. Now, Nathan was never really shy about it. If anything, he was more than willing to tell you how he felt or how he was dealing with it. He talked to my husband many times throughout the years about how to get into the computer programming in order to fulfill his dream of making video games and art. He wanted to do well in the world and have a future, yet there seemed to be a disconnect between his dream and taking the steps to make that dream a reality. When it came down to it – he just seemed lost. Despite all the help, love, and support he received, this dark cloud followed him into adulthood.

We had both moved away from home to live our own lives, and for the first time in a while he seemed determined to start the steps he needed to take to get himself together. We continued to keep in touch despite living half a country apart. We texted about video games and shared pictures of our artwork. He still talked about re-registering for college. We would talk about movies we wanted to see and shared little tidbits of our lives here and there. Isaac and Nathan also grew close; they would play Xbox Live together, teaming up against fantasy foes and forming their own sort of virtual relationship. I was continuously trying to convince him to move closer to me, but to no avail. Why am I sharing all of this? I suppose to set the stage for what I'm about to share. Nathan was so excited for us when we shared our pregnancy announcement! Here's our text conversation:

> Nathan: *That's amazing Devin I'm so happy for you*
>
> Me: *Thank you little brother*
>
> Nathan: *It's nothing Devin. I love you so much. I'm so happy God chose you to be my sister.*
>
> Me: Awe *thank you. I love you so much. I've always thanked God for how close we are. Love you so much.*

As I look back now, I feel Nathan was trying to say goodbye. After his last response, I had picked up my phone and started typing more to him. I had wanted to ask if he was doing anything for Halloween, but I was distracted. We were at a restaurant and the waiter came to take our order, so I never sent the text. I'll always wonder what would have happened if I asked him that question. Would it have made a difference? Would he have shared his intent or feelings? Would he have begun to look at the future? Would I have seen a hint of anything that would have happened that night? The "what ifs" and survivor's guilt can eat you alive if you let it, every time it rears its ugly head. Yet, I also know that no one but himself is responsible for the decisions he made that night.

The next morning – November 1st 2014 – was a Saturday. Like every other Saturday, I went to work like normal. My joy was through the roof; I was growing a baby! We had shared the news with all our close friends and family (apart from Isaac's parents). Our plan was to get off work early and head to my in-laws for the exciting surprise announcement. It seemed like nothing could shatter my joy! Then Isaac walked into my workplace. I knew almost instantly that something was wrong or else he wouldn't be here. He asked, "Can I talk to you outside?" We stepped outside, and my life was changed forever. Nathan had committed suicide the night before, just hours after texting back and forth. I felt as if someone shoved a knife into my gut, and not just figuratively. When Isaac told me, I immediately felt a physical reaction – as if someone had punched me and knocked all the breath from my body.

That night I felt so lost. I didn't know what to do or think. I couldn't just stay home; I needed to run away. I needed to be with my family. I had this disconnected idea that maybe if I ignored this, it would go away. I never hated living so far away from my family more in my life. But, Isaac and I decided to continue our plan to drive to Isaac's parents and tell them about the baby. You might be thinking, but why? Truthfully? I just didn't want to be alone. I wanted to be surrounded by as much family as possible. I wanted a distraction. A few hours later, I went to the bathroom and saw blood. No, no, no. Not now. I can't have this now. I took a deep breath and tried to calm myself. I knew I was in a dangerous situation; the stress and grief could cause me to lose my child. But now this child felt like the last connection I had to Nathan; it was the last thing we talked about. I know now I would never have recovered if I had lost my son along with my brother—one of my best friends.

I knew I had to keep it together to protect my baby, and I never understood until that moment the true power of the mind and will. I was mourning, broken, and beaten. I felt like my life was ending. Yet I snapped up emotional walls and tried not to let myself be overcome with grief. I let myself feel –I wasn't able to hold back the entire dam of emotions— but I only let so much escape. Every time I became distraught I would shut myself down and think of the baby. The bleeding stopped almost as soon as it came, and I convinced myself it was a fluke thing.

I flew down to Louisiana a few days later to be with my family for a few weeks, hoping to help my parents as much as possible. We had a beautiful memorial service remembering Nathan for who he really was and not who the depression made him to be. After his death, the people Nathan positively impacted seemed to come out of the wood work. We learned more about him than we ever knew. He was a beautiful soul, and I think my parents put together a memorial service that would have made him happy.

The next morning I woke up, went to the bathroom, and discovered blood everywhere. It was as if time stood still and I disconnected and exited my own body. I remember thinking, "Stay calm just breathe." The irony of life and death did not escape me. I was here mourning the death of one while yet holding onto hope and praying continued life for the other – two completely opposite forms. After rushing to the emergency room, the first doctor couldn't tell me anything about what was wrong; I felt dismissed and ignored. I was given a report of the ultrasound images along with a bunch of pamphlets on miscarriages with information including the early signs, the percentages of every pregnancy, coping groups, etc. They couldn't say for sure I was losing the baby because as of now there was a very strong heart beat. Yet, because I was bleeding and still early in my pregnancy (about 8.5 weeks), I needed to know miscarriage was a possibility. They said to come back if the bleeding got worse. The next day the bleeding became so severe I was filling a pad every two hours and passing huge clots. This was more blood then I had ever seen in my life, more than I'd seen even during my periods. I began to prepare myself for another loss. We went to the Emergency Room again, but this time I had a very knowledgeable doctor who allowed me to hear a strong, beating heart and see a little baby who happy and content, somersaulting all around. But, the ultrasound also showed something else; I had a subchorionic hemorrhage. This is when the gestational sack pulls away from the wall of the uterus and causes a hemorrhage. The doctor told me that the bleeding would continue until my body was able to heal the hemorrhage on its own. In my case, I bled very heavily and consistently until eighteen weeks of pregnancy, then on and off again until my 3rd trimester. Knowing what the bleeding was helped me to stay calm, but what helped the most was feeling my baby moving. I also received extra monitoring which helped put my mind at ease.

I never felt that I could actually grieve the loss

of my brother as I went through my pregnancy. I was so cautious of everything and was constantly afraid the emotional stress would cause me to lose my child for whom I had prayed so long. I felt it couldn't be a coincidence that the bleeding started immediately after Nathan's death. Yet, looking forward to a miracle, feeling him move, and watching him grow allowed space for joy in the middle of my deep and horrible loss. Anyone who has ever lost someone can tell you that grief doesn't go away; years later that loss is still deeply felt by my entire family. Perhaps grief is best described like a winding road. Most of the time you're moving along with life when a sudden curve reveals grief sitting right there, waiting to remind you of its presence. It has never left.

Chapter Eight

Fair warning! If you have a weak stomach, go ahead and skip through my birth story in this chapter. As you can tell from what you have already read, I am anything but shy when it comes to personal information. Proceed at your own risk!

All right – let's just make sure we are on the same page from the get go. Birthing a child is a beautiful yet disgusting and painful process. It's a two-for-one deal. Now of course the outcome far outweighs everything that we have to go through, but yes, it is most certainly not always this magical moment we hope to experience. Like most young, soon-to-be moms, I prepared a step-by-step birth plan for my team that included everything I wanted done. I made all my plans as if my body would magically respond how I wanted it to respond. I can tell you now – this was a beautiful waste of time. If you aren't catching my drift – my birthing journey was not easy and did not go at all like I had hoped! The biggest things I am forever grateful for is that my mom flew in just in time for the birth (literally within a few hours) and was able to come straight from the airport to the hospital and that my amazing husband didn't leave my side the entire time.

It seemed my little man was ready to come into the world three days before my due date. At 4:45 AM on a Wednesday morning in June, I rolled myself over in bed (feeling much like a turtle on its back) to go to the bathroom – no easy task when you are forty weeks pregnant! I felt a big POP as I rolled. At first I thought my little guy gave me a huge kick, but when I stood up and suddenly had a waterfall flowing down my legs, I knew my water had broken. It was time! I yelled to Isaac, "Wake up!" and I don't think I have ever seen him move so fast. I swear that within a two-second span he was up, dressed, and ready to go. He told me he had just finished a dream about my water breaking! We both laughed about how maybe God was trying to prepare him mentally for what was to come.

I wasn't having contractions yet, but I called the hospital to see when they would like me there. I was asked to come within two hours. Unfortunately, I had previously tested positive for Strep B, and they wanted me on penicillin as soon as possible to make sure I received at least two doses before birth. They told me to eat because I wouldn't be allowed anything once I got to the hospital, but I was way too excited!

The food Isaac placed before me tasted like sand. I would eventually wish I had devoured as much as could possibly fit into my body. There are many reasons for that and I'll list just two for you. First, my body was about to have the biggest workout of its life, and I needed the energy. Second, I had no idea how long this process was going to be! In my naive little mind I was going to go in and pop out a baby within a few hours. So after a few bites of eggs I was ready to go!

Upon arrival, they confirmed my water had indeed broken. I was measuring 3 cm dilated, -1 station, and about 70-75% effaced. I know a lot of you will read that and have no idea what it means. In laymen terms, I wasn't having any pain or discomfort, yet my body was already making great progress. They went ahead and checked us into a room, and I began to do anything I could to help progress, including lots and lots of walking. Within a few hours I was finally beginning to feel contractions as I walked the room. At 3:30 PM, they checked again and I was now 7 cm dilated, 90% effaced, and 0 station. It seemed things were progressing really nicely. I was still not in a lot of pain. I had been preparing for this for the last twenty weeks. Anytime a contraction hit I would use a mediation technique to let it all go, and I was still able to smile after every contraction. The nurses where amazed as they watched the waves on the screen rise and saw me close my eyes and breathe through it without making a sound. One young lady who was in residency for midwifery wanted to learn all about what I was doing; she had never seen anything like it. I felt so proud! How on earth had I gotten this far with so little pain? I felt like a super woman and knew my birth plan was going exactly as I desired. Now – queue the dun-dun-duh music at your leisure.

At 9:30 PM there was still no baby, and things came to a terrifying stall. I began experiencing immensely painful contractions lasting about two minutes each and coming in one-to-two minute intervals. Instead of being able to rest, meditate, or even catch my breath, I began vomiting profusely between contractions. Let me put this in perspective – I would experience two minutes of the worst pain I'd felt in my life, then and instead of being able to lay back on a pillow or catch my breath, I would vomit until I couldn't breathe. Then another contraction would hit. It was constant. I was in hell and felt like my body was trying to kill me. I also began experiencing extreme back pain, pressure, and back contractions. I shook uncontrollably to the point that everyone on the medical team believed I was in the transition stage and the baby was coming. They called the midwife in to look and begin the pushing process but nope! Very surprisingly and very disappointingly – I was dilated and effaced exactly the same as I was seven hours ago. This confused the midwife, and she decided to check things out. We discovered my little one had decided he wanted to be able to see all there was in the world as soon as possible. He turned himself face up (also known as sunny side up). For those of you who don't understand what this means, I will try to explain it briefly. Instead of laying on his side or his back, he had turned and his spine was on my spine. This caused extreme pain, and the midwife believed this made me unable to progress. The biggest part of him was trying to come out of the smallest part of me instead of our bodies working together and flowing naturally. I had already been in active labor for eighteen hours, so at this point they asked me what I wanted to do. I wanted to try to continue on naturally. I wasn't opposed to an epidural, but I wanted to see if we could get him to turn back around be so I would be okay. The midwife agreed to check on me in a couple hours to see if I still felt this way. During those two hours nothing changed in either pain, position, or progress. I felt I couldn't even stand because I was so weak.

About this time, my mom walked into my hospital room. I don't think I had ever been happier to see anyone in my entire life! In between vomiting, contractions, and shaking I told her that I didn't think I could do this naturally; I needed medicine. My mom understood, partially due to being in the medical field, and she immediately asked them to give me nausea medication. I wondered why no one had thought of that before - why wasn't it offered? Within thirty minutes of taking it, I could at go at least fifteen minutes without vomiting and was finally able to get some water down, but I was still tired and weak.

I know a lot of you readers are moms already, so my story may be nothing new to you. But keep in mind – I was completely naive about childbirth. The baby's position made it hard to breathe, I began to get dizzy and felt tingly all over. The midwife came in to check progress a few hours later, and once again nothing had changed. This made almost nine hours of being in the same position with nothing to show for all the pain. She informed me that we were reaching a dangerous time. We needed things to progress for the safety of my child. I would need bed rest, an IV, and medicine to help speed things along. She asked again what I would like in terms of pain management, and I told her I needed an epidural. It was honestly something I never thought I would ask for, but after sharing this information the look of relief they gave me was evident. They couldn't believe I had waited as long as I had! Within thirty minutes the anesthesiologist was in my room to administer the epidural. When I say I felt immediate relief I truly mean I felt immediate relief; my pain went from a ten to three! I was able to sleep off and on for a few hours while they had me laying on my side with my legs spread apart by a giant peanut ball. They needed the baby to turn.

At 6:00 AM the hospital shift changed, and I was introduced to my new midwife for the next day. It had been twenty-four hours since I arrived. I had already gone through two different team shifts and was about to be joined by the third and (hopefully) final one. I was beyond ready for this baby to be born! Ironically, the new midwife was the one who had taken my call the day before when I called to say my water had broken. I had been in active labor for twenty-five hours. I had been able to rest for at least a few hours since getting the epidural. She asked if I wanted to keep sleeping or if there was anything she could do for me. I told her I wanted her to check me and tell me I had at least progressed some. It seemed nothing had changed since yesterday regarding my position or dilation, and I just needed to know things were moving forward. She lifted the sheet and gasped, "Um, his head is right here. I think your ready." I just had to laugh!! Here we were not able to do anything, and little man decided in the calm and quiet to get himself ready for pushing. However, in the stubbornness still evident in him to this day – he had not turned; he was still sunny-side up. This would be hard, but my midwife had delivered children sunny-side up before; there would be no need for a C-section. Thus the pushing began.

I will tell you guys (to the mortification of many) that I asked for a mirror. I wanted to see it. No, I needed to see it. I needed to see myself pushing to motivate me to keep going. I was tired, and I wanted to see the miracle of my son's birth. I watched as I worked with my contractions. I would push and push, and he would come out only to go right back inside. My midwife saw my futile efforts and tried to turn his face a little, but he would just move right back to where he was comfortable. For some reason, his comfort was having the biggest part of his head and face in the smallest part of my exit. After about an hour and a half, she made me stop pushing. She said, "Devin, I don't believe in episiotomies. I have only done one in my entire career because I think natural tearing is so much better. But, you are tearing badly and are about to tear straight through your clitoris. Since he is still sunny-side up, it will get really bad and really messy if I don't do this." That was all I needed to hear. She quickly pushed the mirror away from us saying, "I promise you are not going to want to see this." She then cut me on both sides in order to give little man more room to come out. Apparently that was all he needed because in two more pushes he was out! I was holding my beautiful baby in my arms.

I was amazed. He came out silently, not crying at all but with eyes wide open and already looking at everything around him. He was trying to take in everything. As I ooed and awed over my little one, the midwife began to massage my stomach and prepare for the delivery of the placenta. Suddenly I felt a pop and a gush from the inside of my body accompanied by, "Shoot! You are going to hate me!" Just like that, I knew exactly what had happened. I looked her in the eyes and asked, "It broke in half, didn't it?" After confirming, she told me my options were to rush into surgery under local anesthesia or to let the on-call doctor do a manual extraction. After twenty-eight hours of labor, there was no way I was going to be taken from my child and placed under anesthesia. I told her to do the manual extraction.

They say people remember traumatizing moments in severe detail, and I remember everything about this moment. It is imprinted on my brain with sordid detail. The doctor walked in covered head-to-toe in something resembling a HAZMAT suit. Notably, he had on gloves that reached to his elbows. He explained he was going to go into my uterus to scrape the placenta out by hand. He would make sure they got it all out and that there were no hemorrhages. For those of you who don't quite grasp the reality of what this means, let me explain it in further detail. I had just had a baby a few minutes ago. I had delivered this baby turned. I was torn and cut up in a way that, quite honestly, I have yet to fully recover from. I was sore, bleeding, and wounded. This doctor planned to stick his entire arm (yes arm!), fingers, and hand up to his elbow, INTO my uterus and then move it all around like a night at the disco to scrape out the placenta and other leftovers. Sounds like a fun time doesn't it?

I remember being held down as I bucked against the bed screaming at the top of my lungs. This of course didn't help the situation as I'm sure my involuntary response also caused the poor doctor's arm to either get stuck or struggle to do its job. I remember hearing him say, "Just breathe. Do your mediation.

You were doing so good with it during labor; this will be over soon." I remember the pain was enough that I felt on the brink of passing out. And then just like that it was over. When he was done his bright steely blue/silver eyes looked straight into mine. I immediately responded by telling him, "It is a good thing you're covered head-to-toe so I can't identify you, because I'm pretty sure if I ever met you on the street I might feel the need to go on attack mode." I suppose this response could only be expected after all I had endured! They all laughed and thought I was joking. But to be honest at the time I'm not quite sure I was.

After that moment I was finally able to hold my beautiful little man without interruption – or so I thought. Suddenly, my arm began to hurt in a way I had never experienced. I kept telling the nurses throughout the next few hours that something seemed wrong, but nothing *seemed* amiss. Then I looked down, and my arm was blown up to about three times its size. I called my mom over and she immediately called the nurses. It turned out that sometime WAS wrong. Over the last couple hours, the IV that was pumping antibiotics and re hydration into me had either ruptured my vein or pulled out completely, and the liquid now free flowing into my arm caused it to swell. They immediately disconnected the IV and told me there wasn't anything to do but wait as my body re-absorbed everything. After a few hours of discomfort it went back to its normal size, and I hope to never relive that experience. That, my friends, is my miracle baby's wonderful birth story. This child we prayed for caused me to endure what I felt to be similar to hell on earth. My beautiful son to this day is such a joy and precious treasure; and was/is worth every second of what I endured. Even as a toddler he can make me laugh like no one else!

Chapter Nine

About eight weeks after he joined our family, I was hit with a tirade of very hard emotions. As I took pictures of my beautiful bundle of joy and started a group text to share with family, I automatically would add Nathan. Moments like this caused the reality of his loss to hit. All the emotions I had denied, ignored, or put on hold for the safety of my child began to leech through the inner walls I had erected. It felt like I was losing him all over again, but I also felt for the first time that I was allowed to be sad in order to let my healing begin. I believe that my son's arrival caused the healing process to begin as smoothly as it did. I say "begin" because you are never truly healed from a devastation like this. I lost someone so dear to me in the mist of gaining what I desired most in life. I had someone to watch over and distract me when those grief waves would hit. I didn't ignore them this time, but I had a child to care for and smother in love. Watching my son grow and seeing his personality emerge is one of the most amazing things I have ever witnessed. Each smile, each laugh, each new stage in his mental development was beyond amazing and exciting to watch. Even now my family and I get so much joy watching him explore the world and find his individual self.

My period came back in full force twelve weeks after giving birth. I was mortified! It was the last thing I wanted to deal with, and since I was breast feeding I had hoped it would keep away for much longer. Before our little man came, we decided we would never want to do anything to prevent a pregnancy after his birth since it had taken so long to conceive him. Yet, the thought of having another child so soon after giving birth was overwhelming. Let's be honest here (and I know all you moms will be raising your hands and shouting, "Amen!" at the top of your lungs) – babies are HARD! You feel like you lose a huge piece of yourself - which is worth it – but the baby stage is also one of the hardest seasons of motherhood you will ever have to go through. We had worked for years to bring this little one into the world. How could I open myself up to try again when pregnancy alone sapped the strength from me? I felt I needed to give my son 100% of who I was; the idea of having another so soon was beyond me. For now, I wasn't willing to share my attention with anyone else. When I told Isaac we needed to buy condoms, I remember the shock and disappointment that seemed to echo from him. He reminded me of all we had gone through and reminded me that we had said we would never prevent again. As he shared his desire for more kids, we had a long, hard, and honest discussion about where I was at emotionally and physically. I wasn't ready for another child yet, and I didn't know how long it would take before I would be.

Despite his own desires, Isaac supported me as

always. I knew I needed to do what was best for myself, and he never once pressured me to change my mind. Eventually my mind unexpectedly changed on its own much sooner than I expected it to. When Ezekiel turned four months, the idea of another baby didn't scare me like it did just a month before. Our infant was beginning to adopt lovely sleeping habits, so our lack of sleep didn't feel as life-siphoning as before. While I wasn't ready to actively pursue another child, I thought that we could do away with protection. As the months went on, I started to really want this to happen; we wanted another child. Once again, Isaac and I sat down for a discussion. What should we do? Do we begin fertility treatments again? Move into adoption? Try to get pregnant on our own? I didn't want to endure the fertility treatments and monitoring again. I didn't have the stamina, emotional readiness, or drive for it. We decided we would begin actively trying; charting and timing intercourse on our own like we did before. Since we had already delivered a full-term child…maybe future pregnancies would fall into place for us. We both agreed too that adoption was definitely in our future. Regardless of if we conceived again or not, once our son turned two we would begin the adoption process. I can't say why we settled on year two. Maybe we didn't like the idea of years going by with only one child? Regardless, "two" was the number neither of us could get out of our heads. We felt led to be parents to a houseful of children, and whether that happened through natural means or through adoption didn't matter to us.

Thus we began our active journey to get

pregnant again. I charted my cycles and we timed intercourse as close to ovulation as we could. Noticeably, I didn't have a devastating feeling when my period returned month-after-month. I had my miracle baby, and as much as I wanted another child I found so much comfort in the one I already had. It is not lost on me that this is not the case for many of you, and I can tell you my heart has not forgotten what that feeling is like – I weep with you.

As time went by, my charting revealed this would not happen on its own. If we wanted another child, we needed some kind of medical intervention once again. Still, I was unwilling to put myself back through the emotional turmoil and financial stress that came with the reproductive endocrinologist. One of my friends recommended her OB-GYN; since I had gone through this already, her OB-GYN would be willing to prescribe the fertility medications I needed without the extra tests and monitoring. I will be honest – I felt torn. Part of me wanted to give it a try while the other part was happy where we were. We knew adoption was in our future, so could that be enough? When I talked with Isaac, I could tell he was thrilled with the fertility option; he really wanted this. He showed me that no harm could come through talking with the doctor and hearing his thoughts. Yet after every conversation we had about biological children, we would proclaim to each other that this wouldn't keep us from adopting in the time frame we had already discussed.

I called my friend's doctor and found that he had a six-month waiting list for new patients. I was actually okay with this and booked myself an appointment for as soon as possible. I figured this would give me time to get pregnant or change my mind. Life then seemed to carry on as normal. We continued with timed intercourse while never really expecting it to go anywhere. Little Man turned one, and we took a family vacation to the beach. That was such a fun trip that brought so much joy from seeing our little guy exploring his world. While on that trip, I began to feel off. I started getting heartburn every night so badly it would make me want to vomit. Toward the end of the trip, I became nauseated after a few bites of food. My heartburn and nausea continued after returning home. I began to wonder if we were miraculously pregnant! I raced to the store to buy a test.

While I was taking that test I kept telling myself not to get my hopes up. We had been trying to get pregnant on our own for three years, so there was no way this would be positive. When the second pink line suddenly appeared on the test, I entered a state of shock that caused me to freeze as I stared at the test. I didn't really think this would happen. After all this time how was this possible?! I called my mom and sister and sent a text to my most intimate friends. In that instant, I realized how badly I really did want this. Before this positive test, my feelings were torn from being willing to put myself out there again. But now a pregnancy was here, and I was over-the-moon excited!

****Trigger Warning****

A week later, I relived a nightmare as I began bleeding and once again lost my child. There were differences. I felt very torn as I battled a large variety of conflicting emotions. On one hand, for the first time in almost four years I had gotten pregnant on my own! This gave me hope and peace that God could give us another child if He really wanted it to happen. On the other hand, there was disappointment. I had been happy for the briefest of moments, and then just like that it was gone. I told Isaac I thought I might cancel the appointment I had with the OB-GYN for the fertility medication. My argument was that this pregnancy showed us we could get pregnant on our own. I was experiencing the very large difference between getting pregnant on my own versus via mood-altering medications. I didn't want to relive the emotions and the crazy that came with the fertility medication hormones. However, Isaac expressed his heart and shared that he really didn't think we would be able to do it on our own. At this point, we had either been trying to get pregnant or to stay pregnant for almost five years. Our most recent loss had shown him how much he truly wanted another biological child. He acknowledged that it was ultimately my decision. I love my husband. I love our son. I loved both the babies we had already lost – so much. As I examined my feelings, I knew I wanted another one. The loss of this pregnancy made me realize just how much I really did want it.

October arrived and with it my appointment. We went over my file from the Reproductive Endocrinologist and talked in depth about my history. The doctor was comfortable enough to prescribe me medication without requiring the prodding, poking and analyzing that the Reproductive Endocrinologist did. I left that day with a prescription in my wallet, but suddenly I was hesitant to take it. Timing wasn't the most convenient. We had two family trips planned, and we would be sharing hotel rooms. If the required intercourse happened to fall during that time then we were basically wasting a whole cycle. There was no way I would kick my mom or sister out of the room in order to fulfill our duty (so to speak). Plus, I was still holding onto the hope that maybe I could get pregnant on my own, and I still wasn't ready to deal with the hormonal ups and downs of the medication. Neither of us had any doubt that this was going to work for us when we did start. It was just a matter of doing so. Two months later, I followed the elusive white rabbit down the rabbit hole and once again began medicating.

The first month brought disappointment. We didn't see the results we were hoping for, but I reminded myself that last time the first month did nothing as well. As optimistically as I could, I pushed past this and moved straight into the second month. We received a positive pregnancy test this round, and oh my goodness we were so excited! Here it was! Because we used the magic pill, we knew we were going to have this baby! I called the doctor's office to see about getting extra monitoring due to my two previous losses, and they asked me to get blood work every couple days for a week to see where my pregnancy hormones (beta numbers) were and to monitor how they grew. I probably checked my phone twenty times a day to make sure I never missed a call about those numbers. They continued to rise at every call, and I felt more peace. By the end of the week, they told me that while my numbers where technically in the normal range and were continuing to grow, they were a little low compared to what they like to see. Yet, this didn't necessarily mean anything. They said I should probably wait another week and come back in for one more test. I declined. We knew that in a week if the numbers went down I would miscarry whereas if they continued to go up things would move forward. Regardless, I wanted to enjoy the life-changing miracle that was here without fixating on what the next test would say. At this moment – I was pregnant. In a week I would know one way or another if I was going to lose this baby too. In an act of faith, I called and booked my five-week appointment with my previous practice and set everything in motion.

Things seemed to happen really fast during the first few weeks of pregnancy. I was grateful for the nausea since it pointed to everything going just as it should be. At my five-week appointment, my doctor told me that everything looked wonderful. I was obviously pregnant and my HCG levels were high and good. This was the best news we thought we could ever receive; it was really happening! We were having another baby! What really amazed me was that I began to show immediately. I'm not talking about a bloat bump, but an obvious pregnancy bump. In fact, I had begun to grow so fast that I seriously wondered if there might be two in there.

Naturally, I began nesting, organizing, and rearranging. Since we knew adoption was in the future, we wanted to have things rearranged as soon as possible. Our plan was for Ezekiel and the new baby to share a room so we could still have a guest bedroom or a room for another child (when the time came). However, when we received our due date we realized that this baby would be coming at the same time we would be having another child join our family.

Memories of the first several months with a newborn surfaced, and we began to question the wisdom of our plans. Maybe we needed to wait another couple years. Maybe we should wait until this new child turned two before we continued. It wasn't set in stone, but it was a plan we began to kick around internally.

At home, things began to progress as you would expect with something as exciting as this! We picked out names, painted the bedroom, and even began moving Ezekiel into the new room he would share with his new brother or sister.

A few days after turning nine weeks, I went to the bathroom and discovered some light bleeding. It had come out of nowhere. My heart jumped into my throat. Locking myself upstairs, I called my midwife to see what I should do. While I waited, I reminded myself over and over of all the bleeding I had with Ezekiel. I reminded myself of all the names of people that I knew who experienced the same thing. I probably repeated this to myself about twenty times: "There is no cramping, I feel fine." After what felt like an eternity, my midwife got on the line and assured me it could be normal but that it could also be something else. She told me straightforwardly that if I was loosing this baby, there really wasn't anything they could do for me this early. She told me to call her back and head to the emergency room if the bleeding got heavier or cramping began. I tried to tell myself that this wasn't going to happen. I tried to go about the rest of my day as if everything was normal, yet my mind screamed at me that my body was failing me once again. Even if nothing was wrong and the baby was fine, the reminder that this life was not guaranteed hung over me like a dark cloud.

That night I began to having actual contractions. I recognized them immediately. I also began passing huge blood clots. In that instant I knew that we were losing the baby. I shut off my emotions much like when I lost Nathan. I knew what was coming. I knew nothing could be done. I called my midwife and told her I going to the ER. She set up a follow-up appointment for the next day in case I was wrong. I didn't want to go to the hospital alone. However, since we had no family here and our toddler wasn't even a year old I wasn't sure we had another option. I didn't want him there with me as I was losing my child. I contacted as many friends as I trusted in this vulnerable moment in order to get someone to come over and stay with Ezekiel. Unfortunately, none were available to help, so after about thirty minutes of contractions worsening and continued bleeding I left on my own to go to the hospital.

I knew what was happening, but I still tried to come up with any other plausible explanation. Maybe there are twins and I'm losing one of them; after all, I looked about four months pregnant but was only nine+ weeks along. Once I arrived at the hospital I tried to keep myself distracted and calm. I wasn't going to let myself be overcome with negative feelings. As I was going through emergency room security, the guard took one look at my stomach and asked me if I knew if I was having a boy or a girl yet? Yes, this is how pregnant I already looked. In that moment it was hard to keep a straight face or give a kind answer. Here I was wondering if I was even going to have a baby when I left the hospital, and this stranger asked me if it was a boy or girl. But, maybe he was right – I didn't know exactly what was happening. I wasn't a doctor; maybe there was hope. I simply responded that it was too early to tell but that I was leaning toward letting it be a surprise.

In a matter of minutes I was signed in and given a wait time of about five minutes. In that moment, it was as if my body realized I was someplace safe so it could do what needed to be done. I immediately began full contractions while bleeding so heavily I filled a pad every five minutes. They rushed me into a room as fast as they could. The bed was lined with similar materials from when I gave birth to Ezekiel, and the irony was not lost on me. I was there having contractions in a room just like I gave birth in but I knew I would not leave with a healthy baby in tow.

The doctors informed me that while they would do an ultrasound as soon as possible, it was likely I was losing the baby. There was nothing that could be done; I was left alone. They checked on me periodically, but overall I was alone with my thoughts in a sterile room. I put on a brave face every time they checked me, but because of the contractions and blood

I knew it was just a matter of time. I cursed myself for coming there; I could have lost my baby at home in this same silence. After an hour went by, all I wanted was to go home, curl into a ball, and cry. I was reminded with each contraction and fresh wave of blood that I was losing my child. I knew there was nothing they could do, so why on earth was I here?

I have re-written this next part over and over, with many tears. I have had to decide what to share about this next moment; I struggled with guilt, anger, and sadness then and now. Part of me has wants to guard my heart and gloss over all details, while the other part of me knows that is not the purpose of this book. The purpose of this book is to tell my story so that others who have experienced the same thing will know they are not to blame, nor are they at fault. In this truth, I tell my story.

As I sat in silence suddenly I felt a huge amount of pressure like I needed to use the bathroom. Almost instantaneously after sitting on the toilet, I saw the entire sack with my beautiful little baby come out all in one contraction. I will never be able to forget that picture; it is forever ingrained on my mind. I stood up in shock, unsure what to do. I watched the entire gestational sack sink to the bottom of the toilet and move out of view. All I wanted was to get home. I had just lost my baby, right there before my own eyes. I couldn't hold him or her. I couldn't even see if it was one or two. I felt that the little bit of closure I might have had was ripped away from me. While I have learned that we can feel sadness and betrayal within our bodies we should never carry guilt, I still struggle to forgive myself for letting my baby fall into the toilet while I helplessly sat.

I washed my hands in a daze and went back to bed where I called the nurses and told them what happened. They still wanted an ultrasound to make sure there was no retaining tissue, but I knew there wouldn't be. I saw everything that came out. I knew I lost everything. I updated Isaac via text, and this was one the hardest parts for me. I was glad he wasn't there to suffer with me, yet at the same time I wanted him there.

After almost two hours of waiting, the ultrasound tech arrived and confirmed that I had indeed lost everything. In fact, my lining was back to what it should have been per-pregnancy. I went from bleeding profusely to merely spotting within the hour.

In these moments, something inside of me broke and has yet to heal. If I'm being honest sometimes I wonder if I didn't want to heal because healing would mean I have to put myself back out there. I knew in that moment that I was done. Never again would I trust my body to carry another child. I had been pregnant four times and only had one child. I had no inclination that anything was wrong with this baby, yet I had just lost a piece of my world.

I was released after making a follow-up appointment for a few days later. But because life is cruel (but not all people) that same security guard looked at me on my way out and kindly asked how everything went. I immediately broke down and for the first time said it out loud – I had lost my baby. There it was. It was real, and there would be no denying it. My body still told a different story. I still looked pregnant, and almost everyone still thought I was pregnant. Our home still had rooms set up to welcome our new little one. I still had a baby blanket that I'd begun to knit. But my baby was gone, and nothing was ever going to change that.

Chapter Ten

At some point that night I needed to use the bathroom. Isaac was waiting for me when I came out and wanted to know if I was okay. I was hit with an emotion I had not experienced in a long time. I wasn't quite sure what to say, I wanted to explain something I had never realized before. This was the first time in almost five years that I had used the bathroom without analyzing what was coming out of my body. There were no mind games. "Is this really my period? Maybe it's implantation bleeding or ovulation spotting. Maybe I'm not really miscarrying, etc." I knew I had miscarried and while I felt grief, I also felt a strange sense of weight being lifted off my shoulders. Looking back, I can see how God was working – even in those moments of despair – to bring me where I am now.

I went to bed numb and exhausted and began sobbing into my pillow. I knew Isaac was walking through this with me, yet he was experiencing it in a very different way. I felt lost and alone. I felt God tug my heart. I don't know if I was awake, asleep, delirious, or just tired, but I remember vividly seeing a woman come to our door and knock. We opened our door to two older children, and the woman held book bags containing the children's possessions. They were waiting to meet us and for us to adopt them. I felt God whisper to my soul. We loved this miscarried child so much, yet it wasn't even fully formed. Every day, there were children across the world who woke up feeling unloved, unwanted, and devastated. It was like a switch flipped in my heart. My heart for adoption was unchanged, but now the "who" was different. I now wanted older children, the children who had experienced great loss or disappointment and needed someone to show them hope. I wanted the children who were harder to place. I wanted the children that so many people gave up on on because it would be too hard. Readers, please know it is not my intention to tell you that older kids deserve to be adopted more than infants or younger children. I do not take lightly that even infant adoption also has loss. While my heart was leading me to older children, I also knew we had just experienced a huge loss, and I did not wish to push Isaac into something he didn't also feel led to do. If this was going to work, the only way would be together.

You might remember we had planned to begin the adoption process when Ezekiel turned two. After getting pregnant, we knew the timing would not work out as we originally intended. Now the big question that weighed on our hearts was this: "Do we go back to the original time line?" As we considered the best way to process our grief and decide on next steps, we chose to take two months to heal, pray separately, and decide how we each felt we wanted proceed. We didn't want to sway each other as we considered this life-changing decision, and we didn't want to make a decision based on our emotions or loss. Those two months of internal processing were agonizing to me as a verbal processor. I couldn't share my innermost thoughts or emotions with my best friend and supporter! I praise God to this day for friends and family who were willing to let me spew out words as my heart transformed and healed in ways it so badly needed.

We planned a six-hour road trip for our two-month mark. We decided to use this time to talk. I needed to let Isaac go first. I was afraid that if he said anything I didn't like, I would need to take some time to organize my thoughts before we continued. What took place on this ride is proof that a marriage that is God-centered and founded on openness and love can bring two souls to the same place (just maybe not how you would imagine). Isaac shared that he felt we were to move forward with adoption on our original time line. He shared with me that several years ago he felt we should adopt older kids, but he didn't want to say anything to me until this moment. He didn't want his desire to push or pull me. Well, I think my jaw hit the floor! Here I was thinking and praying for God to change my husband's heart toward older kids if this was really what God wanted, when all the while He had changed Isaac's heart long before mine and was simply waiting for me to catch up. Thus the journey of expanding our family through adoption officially began.

Chapter Eleven

We attended orientation with a local adoption agency one month later. This adoption agency was recommended to me through a client who had used them, and she had nothing but amazing things to say about them. While they had an infant adoption program, they also specialized in the adoption of older children and sibling groups currently in the foster care system. These children across the United States are considered special needs children because they are older, have been through trauma, undergone parental rights termination, and/or are currently experiencing this termination process. The passion and love that the social workers had for the children was evident in their voices. They spoke about their organization and history. They talked about what the process would look like, and then they played a video that was made by the children themselves speaking about how and why they wanted a family. Let me tell you – neither Isaac nor I could hold in our tears. Here were thirteen, fifteen, eighteen, and even twenty-one year old kids talking about how they just wanted to be adopted. They wanted a family to support them, love them, and guide them. Some talked about how they just needed help knowing how to accomplish their life goals. Others shared their desire to have family during the holidays. As we watched, we both confirmed that this was for us. Not only did we have peace about going older; our age range seemed to disappear. Since we were a younger couple, we couldn't logistically take on a twenty+ year old. But, we could see ourselves doing thirteen and under, maybe even fourteen or fifteen if the match was really good.

After orientation, our next step was becoming licensed foster parents. We had already known that we would adopt through foster care, so this was the route we had to take. We were already registered for classes, and we began them the next month. I don't want to gloss over this time. The information we received was instrumental in setting us up for success. We learned how to parent a child coming from a hard background. We obtained insight as to how to figure out who would be a good fit for our family. We received firsthand training on appropriately reacting when dealing with trauma, behavioral challenges, cognitive development, and so much more! It was also in these classes that we made connection with like hearts who were reading to serve these kids coming from hardships and trials. It opened us up to an entirely new world full of support and everyday superheroes. We are so grateful to this day for these relationships we still have.

One thing I have found is that the adoption journey truly isn't for everyone. I used to think (incorrectly) that anyone could adopt. I could not believe that some people would not want to adopt. Yet, the fact of the matter is not everyone should adopt. This journey is certainly not for the faint of heart! It requires not only a desire but also a calling and a willingness to work around broken hearts and the hurts that come with them. There is loss and heartache in every adoption. Yes, even in infant adoption there is loss accompanied by beautifully rich gain. The kids we wanted to give our hearts and our home to had lost over and over – parental rights were terminated or being terminated. They were broken and beaten. I think back to a training session we received called *Welcome to Oz*. This session taught us that we couldn't parent these children as if they had experienced a healthy background. They wouldn't respond the same way; they didn't know we loved them unconditionally. Their survival techniques – lying, stealing, manipulating, defecation, etc. - had gotten them this far. Why should they interact differently with us? Because of the calling we felt and the training we received, we were unified regarding what we could and could not handle within our family.

After our final class, we were beyond excited to move forward into the home study process. In fact, right after completing the class (which was an hour away from our home) we went straight to the adoption agency to turn in every single certificate, background check, letter, etc; that they still needed. We wanted to do this in person rather than through the mail; we felt this was the most precious information we had ever handed over. A few days later, we were assigned a social worker and were ready to move forward. Our assigned worker had taught one of our training sessions, and she was the one that spoke to us at our orientation. We could quite literally feel the love she had for these kids. I found out later that she had called "dibs" on us at orientation because she could see our serious pursuit and love for these kids.

Now how can I describe the home studies to you? I think the easiest route would be to describe it as someone putting everything about you under a microscope – your life, your marriage and all your family relationships. Nothing is left hidden and no stone is unturned. You can be sure that any unresolved issues in your life will not only be brought to the light but also acknowledged. Isaac and I now understand why our agency requires this process to be completed before a home safety check. I can only imagine the number of relationships that have been strained by the questions regarding your spouse, marriage, feelings, frustrations, strengths and weaknesses – pretty much any topic you can think of! You are asked to share your opinions about each other while sitting directly in front of your partner. I guess another way to describe it would be as "required marriage counseling" … with a bit more probing.

During these weekly meetings, Isaac and I would find ourselves holding hands in the middle of the session or gradually sitting closer to each other on the couch. At one point we were talking about a really hard subject, and the next thing I knew we were snuggling for comfort as we opened our hearts to this stranger sitting across from us. We began realizing that all of our trials and hardships had truly shaped us into who we were today; they had prepared us for this journey. They gave us strength and empathy for the children we would bring into our home. I'm so grateful that my husband had such a pure heart; he spoke his mind honestly during those sessions even when he thought it might hurt my feelings. When we were asked what we desired in a family or who we thought would be a good fit, we confirmed that we were open to any gender, race, religious background, and most behavioral challenges. We both felt like we wouldn't be equipped to handle special needs or handicapped children with mental or physical disorders. We didn't feel equipped for autistic children either.

Now before continuing, I need to calm the ruffled feathers of a few readers who have kids with special needs. You are superheroes, and I think everyone reading this book would agree on that. Not everyone can do what you do. Not everyone has the patience or even willingness to give what their children require to successfully thrive. Through ignorance and lack of information, we thought we did not have what it took to parent these kids, but boy were we wrong! Looking back, I see how God was working even in the waiting periods. Right around the time our home studies began, we saw a change in our toddler that concerned us. Our little man who had been talking in full sentences before he could walk suddenly wouldn't say a word. We would call his name and be completely ignored. He wouldn't make eye contact. It seemed that he could not see or hear you at times. He began to do dangerous things with no fear, things we would expect from a seven- or eight-year old – not a fifteen-month-old (flips off the couch, running places without looking, etc.) We sought help and answers through doctors, therapists, and so forth. It turned out our little man showed us just how well we could parent a special needs child. To make a long story short, we found out our little man had sensory processing disorder (SPD) and that he was sensory seeking. Right here I know a bunch of you are scratching your heads wondering, "What the hell is that?" while others are nodding saying, "Oh yes, I know it well." Let me describe SPD in the simplest terms I can. Imagine you feel like you need to crack your back. Suddenly, that is ALL you can think about. You will move every way you possibly can to get your back to crack. It takes up all your focus. This was Ezekiel one hundred percent of the time. When it came to sensory input, he had a kind of disconnect from his nerves to his brain. He was too young to figure out how to meet his own sensory needs, so he would shut down the outside world and focus on himself to try to find relief. Some kids grow out of this while others learn to self-regulate and meet their own sensory needs. Our little man has since shown a combination of the two. At three and a half years old he finally began talking in short sentences though with a two-year-old's vocabulary (but we were definitely thrilled with his progress!).

I say the above for an important reason. Our son – who needed to be parented differently then a neurotypical child – opened our minds to the possibility that we could handle more then we originally gave ourselves credit for. It opened our hearts to a whole new world filled with special needs children and the parents behind them.

We told our worker that our age range was between eight and fifteen years old with the understanding that the older the child, the more the match would need to be evaluated. We were also open to taking a sibling pair – up to three children at once. When it came to older kids, we didn't want to bring a child home that could or would not view us as parental figures. We also stressed that having a two-and-a-half year old with special needs meant we needed whomever came into our home to know that a toddler will take up more time and attention than an older child, biological or not. They wouldn't need to feel jealous of this; they should understand it isn't favoritism and the toddler stage wouldn't last forever. Something inside of us couldn't draw a line in the sand and say, "Only this, this, or this." I know and respect that some people need to do this, and I do not knock those of you who have. There are so many who are not comfortable parenting kids that come from certain situations, ethnicity, religious backgrounds, etc., and if you moved forward in discomfort it would be disastrous for everyone.

After about a month we were ready for our

home safety check. This went without a hitch, though I had called to see exactly what they would be looking for. Did I need to paint my baseboards? Should my counters be so clean you could see your reflection? The answer to that, by the way, is definitely NOT. They expected the home to be lived in. All they wanted was to confirm our home was safe and that we met the standards the state had dictated. A few weeks later, our social worker called to tell us we had been approved, licensed, and were ready to move forward with matching. All we needed to do was to read and confirm the information written in our home study that she had written on us. She came to our house early the next morning, and we sat at the table to read our lives from someone else's viewpoint. It was very accurate and yet also eye-opening. Thankfully, everything was written from a strengths-based perspective. Things I saw as weaknesses were seen as strengths by someone else. Our lives where written out to show not only the good, the bad, and the ugly but also to show how all of this gave us the tools we needed to parent adopted children.

After reading the home study and signing the final papers, necessary Isaac headed to work while our worker visited with me for several hours. I won't lie – I felt special and honored because this woman who could very easily dismiss herself and head back to work was instead sitting at my kitchen table, drinking coffee, and letting me get to know her. I suppose it is only fair since she now knew more about Isaac and I than any other person. I asked her if she saw herself continuing in her position for the foreseeable future or if she would branch out into another area of social work. I don't know why I asked that question, but the look that briefly crossed her face made me wonder. I had hit something with that question. I sent Isaac a text after she left and told him the question and the look she gave. I hoped this didn't mean she would be leaving us. A few weeks later I received a text from her stating she had found another job, and our matching process was transferring to someone else. I felt a little heartbroken by this. When you've told someone all of your deepest, darkest, secrets, fears, memories, and dreams, it can (even unwillingly) create a bond. There is no getting around that. Yet, my heart was put at ease when she told me that our new case worker was the same person I had already worked with to set up our classes and clearances; she had even taught a couple of them. At least our new case worker wasn't going to be a complete stranger.

Chapter Twelve

That same day our new caseworker emailed us re-introducing herself and asking if we could meet before diving further into the matching process. We were relieved. Yes, she had our life story to read, and we knew that would give her a good sense about who would be a good fit for our family. Even so, it would put our hearts more at ease to sit down together and reiterate what we were looking for and what our concerns were.

Before going further, I need to explain what the matching process is when adopting through the foster care system. This will probably sound harsh, and some of you might shake your heads in disapproval as I describe it. Unfortunately, I can't tell you this process is a magical moment where you spot your child across the room and fireworks erupt in the background as you find the one meant for you. No great sign from heaven is given. The sad truth of the matter is that the matching process – though exciting - is also very heartbreaking. These children have lost so much, hurt so much, and endured so much. Each available child had a flyer. These flyers reminded me of the lost pet signs you might see around your neighborhood or of a resume trying to show off someone's best qualities. Almost all the flyers are written from a strengths-based perspective and offer a very small glimpse into the child's personality, needs, etc. Reviewing these flyers is the first step. The unfortunate truth is that we sometimes felt uncomfortably like we were shopping for a child, but we kept telling ourselves that finding our child would make this uncomfortable feeling worth it. During training, we learned to read between the lines and look for the hidden information given in the flyers. Let me take a moment to expound. We are all a little damaged, and every one of us reacts to life a certain way because of that damage. As adults, we have (hopefully) learned the necessary coping skills that set us up for healing and success. For a child raised in an unhealthy environment, you can assume that (most of the time) those healthy coping skills do not exist yet. Instead, the child has created their very own way of keeping themselves safe. These coping skills come all shapes and sizes, from lying to stealing, manipulation to aggression, etc. With this in mind, we knew we wouldn't be a good fit for every child. We had to find a child who would safely and securely fit into our family dynamic. We had to read these flyers and trying to interpret what the smiling faces and few sentences were telling us. For example, a flyer stating a child loves animals and wants to be a veterinarian tells me that this child would do well in a home with animals and would possibly be okay with younger children. If a flyer stated that a child should be the youngest in the home, could not be with other children, or had other prominent "red flags," we would know they weren't the best fit for us. We also had a family flyer made for the children's caseworkers. It described our family, who we were, what we liked, etc. If we felt a child would be a good match, our worker would contact that child's social worker and send them our family flyer and home study (the novel of our backgrounds, strengths, and weaknesses). If they felt like we would be a good fit, they would send us the child's full file. This was the hardest part of our matching journey. The files they sent us shared all history known by the state about the child. This ranged from abuse, neglect, the number of times removal from or reunification with their birth family took place, behavioral issues, etc. The list really went on and on. We received so many files from caseworkers who wanted us to be their child's forever home. Every time we had to say "no," our hearts broke a little more. Every time we said "no," we knew it was the right decision not only for our family but also for the child. If we could not provide the support they needed, how could we possibly expect this journey to be successful? If we felt a child was a good fit, we were able to ask questions, creating a back-and-forth with their caseworker. If we wanted to move forward, we would then interview with the workers and the State as potential adoptive parents.

Let me pause to say that if any part of my story is tugging on your heart and you feel you might be called to take on this immense role, I encourage you to meet with a local fostering organization in your county. It is a hard journey that is not for the faint of heart, yet it is one full of rewards. Visit www.adoptuskids.org. You can see some of the children in your state who need a family. If you feel that tug, please do not ignore it. I know this is a little sidetrack, but I honestly don't regret it one bit.

So where was I? We finally sat down with our new social worker, and one of the first things she told us was that she does matching a little bit differently then our prior caseworker. She would send us every profile that came to her for us - even those seemed they wouldn't be a good fit. She would just point out their red flags as they came. After we reviewed this information and talked it over, we would tell her, "Yes, we want more information" or we would say "No" and give our "why." This would help us better understand each other. She would get a feel for who we felt would be the right fit for our family based on our "yes" or "no" answers. We showed her the children we already felt connected with from the Pennsylvania Adoption Exchange website along with flyers and profiles that we had been given when we began this journey almost six months ago. Thus our very own matching journey began.

We heard back about two days later from some of the social workers of the children we were interested in getting to know. What initially began as excitement turned into heartbreak and sorrow as the weeks went by; we had to say "no" over and over again. We had never thought about this part. We were so focused on saying "yes" to our child that we forgot we would have to say "no" to so many more. We didn't say "no" because these kids didn't deserve a home or we didn't love them. I think every one of those kids stole a piece of us that we will never get back. But because we loved them, we knew enough to know that we would not be the family best equipped to help them heal their tremendous traumas and heartaches. Throughout several weeks, we would put our little man to bed and then sit down together on our couch to read files and weep. We wept for the children and their pain. We wept that we would have to say "no." We wanted to hold them in our arms and protect them forever. We wanted them all, but we knew we weren't equipped for most of them. The next day we always hugged each other a little bit tighter. When you read what some of these children have been through at the hands of people they trusted the most, the people supposed to be their sanctuary – it can bring such righteous rage and anger accompanied by deep sadness and pain. I prayed for every single one of those kids we said "no" to. I still pray that they find their forever homes with parents who are equipped to help them through their heartbreak and turmoil.

Chapter Thirteen

After several discouraging weeks, we had said or been told "no" close to thirty times. We had not heard back from about four social workers, and it was looking like this process would be much longer than we anticipated. I don't think either of us will ever forget the day our caseworker called us with the news on a particular match. On February 8 at 2:42 PM, I received a voicemail (still saved on my phone!!) from our caseworker. A caseworker who had turned us down for a child had called her. He said he could not get us out of his mind, and he kept coming back to one of his kids that he felt would be a good fit for us. He felt that her interests and personality would fit right in and wanted to know if we would be willing to look at her flyer. I listened to the voicemail and could tell that something was different in her voice; I could hear the excitement! I immediately called Isaac who said that of course we wanted know more. I called the caseworker and made a joke about how she never left me such a happy sounding voicemail before. She laughingly agreed and said she was excited about this match. She described the child's personality, and it sounded like music to my ears. She was described as sarcastic with a dry sense of humor, a verbal processor who speaks her mind, stubborn yet someone who could make friends easily, and her entire team and all her teachers loved her. In short, she was described as a personality that Isaac and I would expect from any of our children. She sounded too good to be true! My caseworker followed up by telling us that she was older and had an autism diagnosis but was extremely high functioning. Even with this, our caseworker had a gut feeling that this was it; this could work. In that moment I felt no fear – only peace. I told her that given the choice I would immediately ask for her file, but I needed to call Isaac and let him decide.

I remember texting him since he wasn't available for a call and telling him everything our caseworker had described. He absolutely agreed we needed to see the child's file. As we waited, I told him, "I feel from the way they are describing her that this could be our daughter." Of course we had a lot of questions. If she was so awesome and easygoing, why were they still looking for a family? Was it just the autism diagnosis? Was there something else? I remembered how scared we originally were to look at any child with any special needs, and now after our own experiences with our son we both had peace about moving forward even with an autism diagnosis; this said a lot about our growth over the last year.

I constantly checked my email to see if we had received her flyer, yet all I kept thinking was that this could be it. This could be our daughter. Then it happened; the email arrived, and I felt my heart skip a beat when I opened it. I began crying, because there she was. I recognized this young girl's face from the adoptuskids.org website; I had seen her before a long time ago when we had finished our classes and entered our home study. We had seen her flyer before and felt a connection then, but because of her special needs diagnosis and our ignorance (at the time), we had decided not to ask about her. Yet, here she was again, and here we were with a new set of eyes and experiences to see and want her. I will say it again – I cried. I cried because I felt like this was a sign. I cried because I was so afraid Isaac might say "no" even though we had been on the same page up until this point. I cried tears of happiness at the possibility that we found our daughter. I cried because of the goodness of God and how He brought her back to us. I cried because for the first time when looking at a flyer I felt so much peace and a tugging saying this was it. I was so thankful that during this process He had opened our hearts to children with special needs whom others might not feel equipped to parent. We know not everyone can, but I was so grateful that we had another chance.

Throughout this process, Isaac and I had an agreement. Whenever a child's flyer or profile was sent to us, we would not tell each other how we felt until both of us had time to look it over and process. I still think this was one of the smartest things we did during this process. We didn't want our emotions clouding or persuading the other person one way or another. When I sent her flyer to Isaac, it took everything within me to hold myself back. I know I wasn't perfectly silent. With all the emotions I felt as I shared her personality description, it was so hard not to notice that it seemed they could be describing our biological child's personality. As I waited for Isaac to get back to me, I called several family members and a few friends to process these intense emotions. I didn't want to influence Isaac with my excitement or thoughts, so they were my safe outlet and sounding board. I don't know if they realize just how instrumental they all were during this process; even just listening was helping. Though I was limited on what I was allowed to tell them, I told them what mattered most - I really felt this could be our daughter. I didn't know why, but I'd had an immediate connection to her face; I felt so much peace with moving forward. I tried to patiently contain myself as I waited, and he didn't take very long. Within a couple hours, we had talked, and we both felt we needed to get to know this young lady.

We called our social worker and told her we wanted to see where this led. She said she would get the file to us the next day and that we would talk after the weekend. The timing of it was both a little eerie and a little perfect. We had planned to travel to visit the same friends we visited after our miscarriage a year ago. It was at their house where Isaac and I had had the conversation about moving into adoption; can we talk about coming full circle? We received the file about four hours into our drive, and I read it aloud from my phone. Once again we felt an amazing connection to this young girl, but we realized the original flyer must have been old; she was older than we thought. She was fourteen, just a month away from her fifteenth birthday. Fifteen – could we really do that? For some reason, we both felt we could. Since her caseworker had approached us feeling we would be good parents for her, we felt more confident in our ability to do this. We had said from the beginning that we were willing to go up to age fifteen if the match was right. But, we had always laughingly stressed that it had to be a really, REALLY good match. For some reason, we weren't even second guessing this girl's age.

We took time over the relaxing weekend to talk, come up with questions and overall wrap our minds around the fact that we both really believed this was it. We unanimously felt there was no reason for us to say "no" and not move toward interviewing with the County/State. We would both look at each other and start laughing randomly throughout the weekend and tell each other we were crazy! Everyone was going to think we were crazy. We both felt the "yes." There wasn't any doubt or a question of feeling like we couldn't do it. Well, at least not yet. We called our social worker after getting back home and gave her the questions we would need answered before moving forward. We also let her know we wanted to talk to the child's caseworkers if possible, and it turned out her caseworkers had requested the same thing. Our social worker informed us that other caseworkers had reached out with other matches, and she asked if we wanted to see those children's flyers now or wait. We both wanted to wait. We felt like this young lady was meant to be with us, and we wanted to focus our attention on her. We scheduled an appointment to sit down with her team to talk. This would give us an opportunity to speak with people who knew her personally, and we could interview each other and ask all the questions we needed or wanted. If we said "yes," we would need to be all in; we couldn't say "yes" and then back away. That would be devastating to any child.

Chapter Fourteen

Even before this meeting I admit that I was already in love. I felt in my soul that we were going to move forward. I saw a lot of myself in this child; she had endured so many things and yet managed to keep a positive outlook. She was so strong and such a fighter; I already felt such a connection. Once our meeting was setup we took time to re-read her file and see if we could come up with any additional questions. We wanted to see more of who she was, what challenges might arise if she was placed with us, and how she would do overall with our toddler (that was our biggest concern). Adoption wasn't just about us; it was about finding a new family member who could adapt, grow, bend and compromise along with all of us. She wouldn't just be saying "yes" to us; she would be saying "yes" to all of us. In case this sounds confusing, know that the older the child the more say they get in adoption placement. This makes sense; the only way a younger couple or family could successfully parent an older child or teen is if the child wants to be on board and make it work too.

I remember the meeting like it was yesterday. It was a cold and nasty day, and looking back I laugh at myself putting on a short sleeve shirt so that it didn't seem like I was hiding my tattoos and trying to be someone I wasn't. I made a joke to Isaac while explaining my choice of outfit; I said that I might as well get it all out there now! Maybe I should even bring a box of wine, set it in the middle of the table, and say "Here I am! This is me. What you see is what you get!" We laughed, but bluntly speaking we were nervous. In fact, I don't think we said more than a few words to each other the entire hour and a half drive to the county office. We were both lost in our own thoughts, questioning how this was going to go down. Once we arrived at the office we found our worker already waiting in the parking lot for us. As we walked towards the meeting we chatted briefly about what the interview might look like and who we would be meeting. We were immediately shown into a meeting room with five other people who instantly put us at ease with their warm smiles and greetings. They were so excited we were there, and their excitement was contagious. In this meeting we were able to get to know this young lady through the eyes of the people who knew her best. I won't go into her history here or later. Though you may be hoping that I expound on her trials, her story is hers to share. Suffice it to say –

we admired her. Our prior feelings about her were coming from a real place. The team answered all our questions as well as they could and helped us feel at ease as we talked to them. We could tell that each of them cared for her deeply; she had a special place in each of their hearts. Now I know I make this meeting sound nice and simple, but I wont lie; this part of the process was awkward no matter how at ease we felt. We asked every question we could think of in order to figure out if we wanted to be with this child forever. I guess you could look at it as being similar to either a blind date or an arranged marriage where you get to ask questions through the eyes of a third party. One big difference is you learn each other's secrets, struggles, and history before you even meet. If we decided to move forward, her team would meet with her as soon as they could to tell her about us, but ultimately it was her decision to meet or not. They felt like we were a great fit and could offer so much to help her grow into a place of healing and confidence, but that they also knew she wanted a home where she could be an only child. She was almost fifteen, so the idea of suddenly having a (very) little brother might not appeal to her. We told them we wanted time to talk and think; we would let them know if we had any other questions.

On the drive home we called our worker (who had left about the same time) to discuss how we felt. She assured us that we did wonderfully and the fact that they basically approved us on the spot was a good sign. They seemed to trust us to handle any challenges that come with parenting a fifteen-year-old. She also assured us that she felt the same thing we did – this could be our match. We told her we would let her know if any other questions came up, but we wanted the next week or two to evaluate our life. We need to think through how we lived our life currently and our responses to various scenarios so we could begin to picture how these things would change if we brought her into our home (if we said yes). We started to use her name openly along with scenarios to see how we would handle certain situations if they arose. You might think, "Okay, wait a minute. You haven't even met this child yet!" Well, the foster-to-adopt program is not like picking puppies from a window to play with for a few hours before deciding if you will keep them. When you say "yes" to foster-to-adopt, you are committing to be parents. Legally, yes – you can back out at any point before finalization. However, each time that happens the child is more traumatized. Yours is another home that has caused loss and broken connections. This can set a child back years in their healing process as they deal with feelings of worthlessness or not being "good enough." Now I know that there may be foster and adoptive parents reading this book and thinking, "I did that. I had to disrupt a placement." Know this information is not meant as an attack in any way; I understand that sometimes a placement must be disrupted for the safety of your family or due to unforeseen circumstances. Maybe you weren't given all the information about what this child actually needed. My point is to reiterate what we are taught in training about continually broken cycles. We knew we had to be thorough with our match before saying "yes" because we could not allow ourselves to do this. It would break the child AND us. This is one reason we loved our agency. Not only were they thorough with the matching process, but they also stressed that when we said "yes," we needed to mean it for better or worse. The more we discussed this the more we realized we had already said "yes" to this young lady in our hearts; our brains were just taking a little longer to catch up.

Chapter Fifteen

A week later we sent out this email to the entire team and county as we officially came forward asking permission to adopt our daughter:

First of all we want to thank each and every

one of you for the parts you have played in

getting us to this point. From the moment we

were sent that email with the flier and the

description of who she is we felt a connection.

That connection grew after the interview we

had with all of you and continued to grow even

more as we took time to reflect on all we

learned from our meetings.

Officially we would like to move forward as

her hopefully adoptive family and have her as

our daughter. We hope this works out so badly

and that she chooses to be with us too BUT we

also respect and agree that she deserves the

right to tell us no if she doesn't feel the

connection is there like we do. Just know that if

she does decide to move things forward we

commit to love her like our own and work with

her from where she is and help her grow to the

highest potential she can while loving and

supporting her all the way. We know there are

going to be challenges along the way and we

also understand that all parties will need to

work together and compromise to make this a

success. But we are ready and willing to fight

for her in whatever way necessary.

We received a reply from her entire team the same day

stating they were excited for us to move forward.

They would meet with our potential daughter soon to

tell her all about us and allow her to decide if she

wanted to meet us. We sent some additional pictures

of us to show her along with our family flyer. They

informed us a week later that they had a date set up to meet with her one-on-one. Whew! Let's just talk about the nail-biting emotions in play. We checked our phones and emails over and over again throughout the day they were meeting with her. Our update finally arrived late afternoon:

Hi everyone,

I just got back in the car. She and I had a great conversation and she is eager to meet you. I shared the pictures with her and we spoke about how we all became connected and our conversation the other week.

She said that she's a little nervous, but it is excited nervous. She had questions and I answered some of them, but I said that others might be best for her to ask you herself, so

she's going to be writing those down.

It looks like we're going to have to schedule a

time to sit down together because she is on

board.

To say that we were nervously excited would be a huge understatement! After spending nine long months in our adoption journey – from beginning our licensing to the matching process – we were here! We could be meeting our future child. The enormous implications were a little lost on us; we were on cloud nine and only thinking of the positive things. Due to our prior discussions with her team, we knew what challenges we might face, but overall we thought it would be easier than we expected. I laugh at myself now when I think back to how unrealistic we were being. Nothing was going to be easy, but all children are worth the fighting for toward success, health, and growth.

This journey – as you will see from continued reading - is messy, complicated, and sometimes very strange. We were thrust into a place of trust and parental leadership while feeling like nothing more than a babysitter (at least not right away). I hope my writing shows the awkward and strange, the laughter and tears, and the ups and downs that occurred. There were times our insides warred as we wondered if we were really cut out for this. We had to remind ourselves and over again that there was nothing wrong with feeling this way. After all, we had been told this was normal for every foster or adoptive parent. You didn't have nine months to bond; you don't have the excited anticipation that comes from birthing a child and knowing they come from you. Instead, you hunt for your new family member only to discover a child that is likely hurting and broken. Instead of crying *for* you, this child will push you away to keep themselves safe. Your new child or children might be at war with themselves, and because you are their safe space and they know you love them, you will also bear the brunt of their every ugly emotion. I can tell you that we dealt with probably every emotion you can imagine from nervousness to anger, empathy, joy, sadness, regret, excitement, and so much more. Yet with all those feelings came an overwhelming sense of peace. We knew we were on the right path. We knew that we were meant to say "yes" regardless of how her decision would turn out for us. I can't explain why apart from believing that God chose us to be her adoptive parents. Let's be honest –two thirty-one-year-olds wanting to parent a teenager required a bit of a miracle.

As we waited for the County to set up our first official supervised visit, our future daughter asked for permission to email us. We were very relieved to hear this! It would give us a little bit of cushion for getting to know each other before we met in person at the most awkward meeting we would attend. Her request was approved quickly, but the County would be on all email chains between us to supervise. They would ensure a comfort level, and I suppose too they would make sure there was no coercion or other wrong conversation. It was a really smart idea, and I'm very glad they do this. It not only protected her, but it also gave them insight to our relationship and how things were progressing.

We were so excited to receive that first email! It was short, simple, and to the point. She heard from her caseworkers that we were "cool," and she was excited to meet us. She wanted to know what we liked to do as a family and what kind of hobbies we had. Somehow, we felt her nervousness through the screen as our email chain began. We emailed back and forth at least once a day (sometimes more) and conversed on various subjects ranging from our favorite movies and music to things from her past (she initiated this). It was amazing to see her personality come out, and we knew this was helping us break the ice. We began to bond with a warrior who didn't yet know her own strength or how far she could go. She had been told for so long that she was who she was, and she wouldn't be anything different. We clearly saw her potential, and we just *knew* we were meant to be her parents. We knew that we were the family to help her meet her full potential. When others saw faults and flaws, we saw the cherished diamond on the inside; this was everything.

Almost a month later (and the day after her fifteenth birthday) the much anticipated day arrived; we finally met in person. Her caseworker was with us in order to help the awkward transition and to supervise. We planned to take her to get a birthday gift, go miniature golfing, and then eat dinner. We had decided that we would not bring Ezekiel during these first few visits. We knew that she struggled with the idea of not being an only child, so we wanted to completely focus on her one hundred percent in the beginning. Chasing a toddler who doesn't know the meaning of sitting still would have divided our attention. Even more than that, we wanted to establish the idea that we would equally advocate for her and for our son; we would love them both. We wanted her to feel close to us before she met him so that any worries or fears she had could be put to rest. We left for this first visit with plenty of time to spare and arrived over twenty minutes early. We were beyond nervous. As we sat at the table, Isaac and I had one of the most awkward conversations ever. Picture a first date conversation between two people who have been married for almost nine years. Neither of us wanted to be left alone with our thoughts or silence. Time seemed to slow down in the most uncomfortable way as we prepared to meet a young lady we wanted as our daughter.

They texted saying that they were there and walking in. My heart began pounding while my leg bounced as if I was in a pogo competition and my life depended on the outcome. I looked at Isaac and words began pouring out uncontrollably like a bad case of projectile vomiting. "What should we do? Do we go to the door? Do we stay here? Do we wait for them to walk to us? Do we meet them halfway?" My lovely husband nervously looked at me and responded as stoically as only a man could, "Okay you need to calm down." I admit that I laughed while writing that out, but only because I know the end of the story. Here we were about to meet our future daughter, and my brain was going a mile-a-minute. I felt vulnerable and scared. I swear that if I had time, I probably would have done several laps around the building to get that nervous energy out. For the entire week leading up to this moment, I was thinking how very similar this felt to a blind date. I never thought I would feel these "first date nerves" or giddiness again. Then they were walking toward us, and this young girl was as visibly nervous as I. I suddenly changed into mama bear mode; all my own fears and worries seemed to vanish. I was determined to do everything in our power to make her feel comfortable. I put myself in her shoes. Here she was, about to meet two people who knew her past and could play a huge role in her future, and she had to decide if she wanted us to be her parents. Talk about a game changer! Once we arrived face-to-face, hugs were given and introductions made. With downcast eyes and a shy smile, she held up a plastic bag holding a beautiful, pink, flowering plant and said, "I got this for you." The ice was officially broken.

We filled that afternoon with window shopping, mini-golfing, and eating. We made lots of small talk. She told us what she remembered about the last time she was here with her birth mother. I responded by saying that I thought that sounded like a nice memory. She looked up at me and said, "Yeah, maybe you and I will make memories together like that in the future." It wasn't a question but a statement. And my heart melted. Did this mean she actually liked us? Did this mean she thought she was going to say "yes" to us? As we spent time together, a connection started taking root. When I look back at our pictures from those first couple visits, I can see the joy radiating off of all of us. We laughed while miniature golfing, making jokes accompanied by lots of awkward moments as we made complete fools of ourselves. For some reason my brain decided to stop working and I kept calling her girl: "You go, girl! Good job, girl! High five, girl!" Yeah...I see you mentally cringing. Believe me – I am too. It's a miracle she didn't say "Nope, I'm out" and walk away right there. During the visit she shared that she wanted to change her name whenever she was adopted. We asked her why she wanted this, and she gave one of the most mature responses anyone could give. She wanted to let go of the past with a completely fresh start. For those of you not familiar with foster care adoptions, note that this is pretty normal because many kids find it a pathway to healing. When they take a new name they move forward with their future and let go of their past. As we sat down for dinner she told us she wanted to move in with us as soon as school was over. We looked at each other and back at her and then over to her caseworker who seemed just as surprised as us. We knew that WE were committed to her one hundred percent, but we had had months to think, pray, and decide before moving forward. We asked her if she felt comfortable with this decision so soon? She said, yes, she knew this was what she wanted; she had made her decision. Needless to say, we were excited but also wary. This was a huge decision for a young teenager to make after only one visit. She started to talk about everything we could do together and places we could go, and we realized she was in a honeymoon period. She was focusing on all the good this change would bring, but she was pushing aside all thoughts of compromise, change, and challenges that would also come with her new life.

Isaac and I looked at each other on the ride home and just smiled. "I guess we have a daughter." "I guess so." It seemed so easy to connect with her; we seemed to click right in together. But of course, nothing is ever *really* that easy, is it? There is no way a story like this could go so seamlessly. We decided the next week to once again meet without our little guy. We wanted to make sure we continued establishing a good connection before pulling him into the visits. This time we went bowling and had lunch. This visit was still supervised, but it didn't have nearly as much awkwardness. We had continued to email through the week to get to know each other. On this visit we laughed and took selfies. She even described how she wanted to decorate her room when she moved in with us. She progressed into making plans for all the things we would do over the next several weeks as we got to know each other. The problem was that all of them were focused on us – no mention of little man. We could tell she was still only looking at the exciting things versus the big picture which included saying yes to him being her little brother. During lunch, her caseworker told her that if she was serious about wanting to move forward quickly, she would need to meet our son. He needed an opportunity to get to know her just as much as she needed to get to know him before moving in with us. We agreed. Time was flying; this needed to happen sooner rather than later. When asked what she thought, she gave a very honest answer. She told us she was scared. She didn't know how to connect with younger kids, and she originally requested a family without other children. From the beginning, we had asked her caseworkers to make it clear that we had a son and also that we desired to adopt again. It would never be "just her" if she said yes to our family. We still wanted a houseful of children. For her, a lot of "what ifs" and unknowns were triggered by our little bundle of joyful energy; it would be a necessary challenge for her to get to know him and form a relationship. She seemed to understand the need to meet him, so we set up our next visit to include Ezekiel.

As we waited for our next meeting, we continued emailing back and forth. This time, she emailed us stating she had been crying all night because she was so nervous. She was worried about what our next meeting would look like. Were we going to separate and spend time with both of them separately, or would we stay together? My heart broke into pieces as I felt her anxiety, worry, and fear. This precious soul had no idea what it meant to have a functional family dynamic. She didn't understand what it meant to do family outings. I forwarded my response to my caseworker and hers because I wanted them to know her fears and reassure her in ways I couldn't yet. How I wished I could have picked up the phone to call her, but at this point we were still limited to supervised visits and emails. I could only pray that our email would do the trick and help to put her fears to rest:

I want to put your heart at ease and let you

know that you do not have to worry. I understand why you would be nervous. This is a very big step. It's exciting too. And this is part of what being a family is. We are going together and will be hanging out together. We aren't going to ignore you and focus only on him and we aren't going to ignore him and focus only on you. We plan on both spending the entire day with both of you at the same time. It might not go perfectly smooth but this will be good practice for all of us to learn how to be together and do things as a family. Now just remember he is only (almost 3) It will just get better and easier too as time goes on and he gets older. So to answer your question we are going all together as a group and will be together the whole time (except bathroom trips

of course) so you don't have to worry we aren't

going to divide up and separate.

It sounds so simple and ordinary doesn't it? Two

parents taking two kids to do something together. But

she didn't know what that looked like. The things we

take for granted everyday can be something huge for a

fostered child. She was grateful for my reply and felt

better about the visit. Either way, I didn't think there

was any way to not be at least a little nervous; she was

about to meet our son. We opted to go someplace

outdoors with plenty of space for our sensory-seeking

son. He could run around, but there would still be

activities for us to do. As the day arrived, though, it

was freezing and wet. We decided to move forward

with being outdoors, but our back up plan for

miserable weather was to go to a mall, window shop, and walk around a little bit. Looking back, my impression of that visit hasn't changed very much. We came with a sensory-seeking two-and-a-half year old who was non-verbal and wanted to see and do everything with the speed of the road runner. We tried our very best to foster any relationship we could between them that day, but let's face it –it went as well as could possibly be expected considering their age gap. We spent maybe an hour outdoors and then decided we were way too cold and miserable to be outside anymore. We headed to the mall to walk around. Looking back, I feel like our little guy did very well under the circumstances, but we also know that she saw him at his worst – over-stimulated, tired, hungry, and cold.

On the second part of our excursion, our teen expressed the desire to do anything and everything that just wasn't feasible. The list ranged from indoor miniature golfing to escape rooms to a movie or even to bowling. All these things were fun, but absolutely not feasible with our young one. It rang another warning bell in the back of our minds. Once again, we saw she was not yet focusing on forming a relationship with our little one at all. She was tolerating him for the sake of us, but we knew that wouldn't work in our family dynamic going forward. She needed to want to be a part of *all* of our lives. Now don't get me wrong – we knew that she was living on adrenaline. For the first time in her life, she saw she was going to have the opportunity to go and do things she never thought she would be able to do. We were giving her a way to not only be part of a functioning family dynamic but also to go on the adventures our family undertakes. She was excited, and that was completely normal up to a point. But we were also seeing a whole lot of, "You guys need to do this for me, and your going to get me this, and then we can go do this." We faced this with determination knowing that one, we could not set her up with false hope about how our family dynamic, and two we needed her and our little guy to bond and see each other as individuals before we could move forward with the quick timeline she had requested.

Chapter Sixteen

We emailed our team after the visit and told them our concerns and what we felt would be the most beneficial moving forward. Going on outings and doing fun things every visit was going to set this relationship up for failure. This wasn't real life; it didn't demonstrate how our everyday life would be. She couldn't see our little man in his own sweetly calm element. Instead, she was seeing him over-stimulated and hard to manage. We knew that her biggest concern was being placed into a big sister role with such a huge age gap, and we wanted the opportunity to show her that we were going to be able to advocate for both of them. With this in mind, we wanted the next visit and all future visits to be at our house. She could come with one of her caseworkers so that she could see what everyday life would be like with us. Everyone agreed that this was the best option, so the plan was set in place. This would still be a supervised visit as we felt that would make it more comfortable. This meant she would be coming to our home (her potential future home) for the first time with people she knew.

When she walked in the door, she looked petrified and very uncomfortable. My heart just broke for her. With shoulders slumped, she stared at her feet, not really talking or saying anything. I asked her if she was nervous and she simply nodded yes. This went on for four or five minutes as she sat on the couch with us in silence. Her caseworkers tried to help us coax her out of her shell and into conversation. Nothing worked. I decided I couldn't take it anymore and asked, "Want to go make cookies?" Those simple words broke the ice! She looked at me and nodded. "Okay come on, how about we all go make cookies." As a family of four, we left the caseworkers behind in the other room as we piled into the kitchen and measured, scooped, tasted, baked, and laughed through the entire process. She got to see Ezekiel in his element; he loves helping Mommy in the kitchen. The visit then continued without any other awkward moments. We hung posters she picked out for her room and played a game as a family after little man went down for his nap. We asked her if she wanted a regular day visit the following weekend or if she wanted to spend the night. She lept at the chance to spend the night – almost a little too quick. We explained that it would be her first unsupervised visit; none of her workers would be with her. Was she really okay with that? She insisted that she was.

The following week, her caseworker called to tell me she was having second thoughts about spending the night. She wanted to do another all-day visit instead. This was a huge step for her, we completely understood that she wanted to slow down. We actually felt that she was making a mature decision. No one wanted to force her to move faster than she was ready. The plan was set, and we emailed her for ideas on what we could do that day. She responded with a simple answer – everything sounded good. Up to this point, we had been emailing at least every day and sometimes two or three times a day. But after this email, everything shifted. I know you can't read someone's mood via text or email, but something in her responses showed me she was shutting down. Maybe it was intuition, but it didn't take Sherlock Holmes to see that her answers became very close guarded with not much give and take.

Sometimes a response didn't come at all. After a day or two of this, Isaac and I sat down to decompress and I began to cry. I told him that I didn't know why, but I felt like she was having second thoughts about us. I cried because we knew that we were who was best for her. I could feel it in my soul – in my very heartbeat – we were meant to be her parents. He told me that I had more discernment over these things then he did, and he I trusted me. We prayed for our daughter who I knew was fighting fear as she thought through the reality of what this move would entail. We prayed for healing and bravery, and for God to open and close doors that needed to be closed. We knew this was not going to be easy. We were trying to give a home to a child who had fifteen years of negative life experiences. We were trying to help her heal but also push her to be who we knew she could be. It is never easy for any age when it comes to something like this, but it's even harder when it's been ingrained for that long.

I received a text from a supervising caseworker Friday evening at 9:00 PM asking which place we were meeting for dinner tomorrow. I was in shock. This was nothing like what we had planned or discussed. We were supposed to have her over all day; I had already taken off work. We had a full day of activities planned, and her caseworker was supposed to pick her up at 6:00 PM. The text hit me like cold water in the face. My intuition was right. Suddenly, there was only dinner for an hour, and it wouldn't even be at our home. I knew she was backing out. I immediately called the visit supervisor for an update; obviously there was miscommunication coming from somewhere. She apologized and didn't know the whole story, but from what she gathered, our girl was having second thoughts. She had originally wanted to cancel the entire visit and not see us at all.

Despite expecting it, this still felt like a slap in the face. Where was this coming from? All month long every visit, email, and daily communication seemed to be going well. Since we now knew she didn't even want to see us, they asked if we still wanted to meet with her for dinner. Our exact answer actually seemed to surprise them. "Until the moment she tells us herself that she doesn't want us anymore, she is our daughter, and we will treat her like she is." We were going to fight for her. She was scared and overwhelmed, and we couldn't do anything to help but continue to love her unconditionally – even at a distance. I cried for her fear, and I cried for the possibility of losing a child I felt I had gained. I cried because of the relief I felt. Yes, that is the part I never expected. While I wanted this so badly and loved her so dearly, there existed a mountain of needs and brokenness. I sometimes worried if we could really do this, despite knowing in my heart we not only could but were meant to. I cried for her pain. I cried because I couldn't pick up the phone to ease her fears or talk her through it. I was forced to go through a mediation system. I was unable to be the Mom I knew I was supposed to be for this young child. And yes, once again I said "child." She was fifteen, but that didn't erase the fact that she still needed a mom, a dad, and a family to love her unconditionally. She needed someone to be there she grew and healed. She needed someone to help her see herself as she truly was –

worthy. She was worthy of love. She was worthy of healing. She was able to accomplish anything she put her mind to.

Though I had scheduled off, I decided to go back to work to distract myself from the suddenly empty house (even though she hadn't been there all week). It was almost the same feeling of the repeated miscarriages. I had looked into her bedroom that morning and seen the posters, decor, and bedding we had all picked out, and I realized she might not be back for those things. At three o'clock, I headed straight from work to the restaurant to meet up with her and one of her caseworkers. Isaac and Ezekiel were going to meet us there. I was so nervous! How do you act in front of someone who may not want anything to do with you? How would I act when all I wanted to do was hold her and never let go? I knew she wasn't ready for that.

I was the first to arrive, and I decided to stand outside so they would see I was already there. When I saw her in the front seat of the caseworkers van, my heart began to race and I wasn't sure what to do. I felt lost without Isaac there. We had always done these visits together, so this was the first time I would be on my own. As they got out of the car and walked towards me, I took a deep mental breath. I noticed the fear and anguish in her body language. Here was a child who had no control over her past, how she was treated, or what she went through. She had now been given choices and the ability to choose yes or no. It hit me that the weight of responsibility would be staggering. Saying "yes" would give her a family, but it was a family she really didn't know yet. From her perspective it would cause her to lose her friends, home, teachers, and even those who had become like family. As adults, we get nervous starting a new job. Can you imagine a teenager facing the decision to start a new life? The fears of what she had endured in the past threatened to come to light if she agreed to not only move in with two strangers but to allow them to become her parents. She would be choosing vulnerability. The magnitude of trust that is required was not lost to me. Plus, there was the additional fact that she would suddenly be a big sister to a child twelve years younger. Even several adults I know would back away at this!

I took a deep breath and prayed for God to lead my speech. I did not want to convince her to come with us. This needed to be her choice. Isaac and Ezekiel arrived and dinner went very well. We saw her begin to relax as time went on, and she asked her worker if she could spend a few more hours with us. Her caseworker was surprised but pleased and gave us permission to take her over to the mall next door. As we got in the car together, I heard with little surprise her statement (spoken fast to just get it out of the way): "I spoke to my caseworker. I might change my mind and not come with you guys after all. I need to think about it more." I was surrounded by so much peace as I stopped the car and looked at her. I told her, "I'm glad you're taking time to really consider this and not rush into it. This decision – whatever one you decide

– is forever, so it isn't something to take lightly." I then specifically addressed the fears she shared with me and asked my own questions to get to the bottom of where some of these fears where coming from. Like I've said already in this book (and you'll probably hear me say it several more times): Her story is her own. I will not go into more details than she gives me permission to share. I can say that the conversation was a good one, and I understood where her fears were coming from after listening to more of her background. By the end of the visit I had so much peace. I didn't know what her decision would be, but I did know that God was in control and all we could do was love her as a family.

While walking around the mall, she talked about things she wanted to do with us over the next several months. It was as if by being with us she forgot all her fear. We answered that these things were too far away for us to commit to right now. We tried to be careful in our wording since we didn't want to give her even more pressure if she realized saying "no" would mean we would continue searching for an adoptive child. We wanted her. We so badly wanted her, but if she didn't want us then we would let her go and move away so we could give ourselves to another child. I know some of you may feel this sounds cruel. Why couldn't we still remain in contact even if she said "no"? The answer is quite simple; it wouldn't be fair to her. She would compare us to other parents and families, and it also wouldn't be fair to our new child who required and deserved one hundred percent of our focus.

Instead, she began making suggestions for next week, but she was once again leaving out our little man. The big sister role comprised a large part of her fears, so we told her that from here on out any visits needed to include our little man if she wanted to see us. We also had to tell her that we couldn't be the ones to make plans. If she wanted to do something next week, she needed to go through her caseworkers and set plan through them.

We spent the next couple hours as a family of four in a fun, relaxed state. We even ran into one of her old teachers! We laughed and joked and were able to see how our family dynamic might look, but we also recognized how much work this was going to be. Even through laughter we saw the hurt that this beautiful soul had endured and how it effected her and inside and out. We had to ask ourselves if we could do it. We knew we were supposed to, and we knew we were meant to. But the enormity of the responsibility hit in waves. We continued to tell our worker that we wanted to move forward as we had peace. We knew things could go either way; she could decide to back out at any moment. But for now, we would be there for her as much as we could. Now the decision was hers.

Chapter Seventeen

I had time to think and reflect on the drive home. I understood completely where her fears came from, and I was able to see through her eyes. This gave me a better understanding of not only her past but also of some things we needed to work through if she decided to move in with us. Isaac and I both pulled into the driveway about the same time. It was late, and our toddler was well past his bedtime. We jumped into parent mode and began the normal routine of putting him to bed. As we read and snuggled with him our hearts were so grateful for a son who was safe and wholly ours. He was a huge blessing; no one would take him from us. After tucking him in, we talked of the day and about the conversation I had with her in the car. We talked about our fears and feelings about where things might go and what we might expect. As we were sitting there, my email chimed:

I guess I want to try.....

So little words yet so much meaning. Just like that, it was as if she had never had second thoughts. She wanted to continue weekly weekend visits. But now,

WE had our guard up. We set boundaries for future visits so she could see our family as it really was. We reiterated with our entire adoption team that from here on out there would be no more activities planned for the weekends – no bowling, roller coasters, mini golf, etc. Since her fears centered around the move and accompanying lifestyle change, we needed to do whatever we could to calm those fears. But how can you calm fears and show how life will be if you aren't living your normal everyday life? We planned weekend visits with fun and affordable things. We packed lunches and cooked dinners at home. The first few weekends seemed to throw her off a bit. We had spent the last month doing fun things every weekend, and stopping caused disappointment. But, it was necessary; she needed to see us in our "natural habitat". Thankfully, she became so comfortable in our home that she asked for an overnight several weeks before she and her team had decided to start them. We decided that if she asked for it, we needed to go for it. We would try one night to see how things went. We hoped that it wouldn't be a complete disaster since it was her idea.

The first overnight went well. We only struggled with one parenting trial- an actual bedtime. She asked what it was, and we both froze (and I mean a deer-in-the-headlights freeze). We were so used to Ezekiel's bedtime routine starting at 7:00 PM, but now we had an older child that definitely had her own opinion about this. Thus the debate and argument about when to go to bed began. I remember with amusement that Isaac and I kept looking at each other, trying to communicate via brain waves and eye contact. I mean come on, they don't exactly teach this in the classes.

Overall, this visit went so well that we began weekend overnight visits every weekend until school finished. Though things were moving forward nicely, things still felt precarious. We weren't her parents, yet we were more than babysitters. It was not easy to navigate the balance of challenging and supporting her while at the same time not coddling or pushing her too hard. As time went on, the mountain that contained years of wrongful thinking was rising, daring us to challenge it. Each new discovery and each new visit made that mountain grow a little higher. It showed us more and more how much harder this was going to be then we initially thought. Yet when Isaac and I sat down and talked about it, we always came to the same conclusion. If these challenges had all been laid out for us at the very beginning, we still would have said yes to her. We knew she was meant to be our daughter, and we are meant to be her parents. She didn't ask for her past, but she was asking for her future. We would fight with her to help her reach every dream she wanted to achieve.

It would be really easy to go down the rabbit hole and tell specific stories and trials that took place throughout our journey. Parenthood in general contains trials and tribulations., and yes, I mean that quite literally. Parenting is hard. You lose a part of yourself with any child that comes into your home no matter how they got there. One of my hardest struggles was being there one hundred percent for both children. But when it came to our daughter I also had to figure out the balance of being the "mom" and being the therapist.

She moved in to be ours forever once school ended. She cried when we met her at the courthouse to become her official pre-adoptive parents. The reality of this step hit her like a bucket of cold water. She was happy to be coming with us and excited for her new life, but she was also very scared. I pulled her into my arms and told her she had every right to cry. This was scary, and this was a huge step. This moment was a stark reminder of the loss that always accompanies adoption. We were excited to gain a daughter, but we were gaining a daughter at the expense of her loss and pain. We once again fortified ourselves and committed to be the best parents we could be to both of our children.

Chapter Eighteen

The rest of this book could get a little uncomfortable for our family. It will also take a turn in writing style. When I began writing, we sat down and talked about what we would or wouldn't include. Our daughter gave us a list of stories she was willing to share, and Isaac and I maintained open communication. I will stick with key points, as there is too much to fit into a book that anyone would want to read.

One of the hardest and most immediate changes we noticed after becoming an instantaneous family of four was the emotional need that both children needed and craved. For the last three years, our toddler was used to being on his own with Mama all day. Now he suddenly lived with another person who was also craving and demanding a mother-child relationship with as much attention as he himself desired. This was beyond his three-year-old comprehension. Sometimes I would be cooking dinner with him on my hip and her snuggling in as close as she could, or I would be sitting on the couch with both of them practically in my lap. She craved the touch she had missed just as much as he craved it for his own comfort. I'm not going to lie. Having a 15 year old who you don't know yet (but consider your daughter) wanting to snuggle with you in a very intimate way can be both awkward and uncomfortable. I knew she needed it. There were times she would almost be sitting in my lap or snuggling in as close to me on the couch as she could and I would have to tell myself not to immediately ask for space. I had to remind myself that she was my daughter and that she needed this touch right now even if I didn't feel intimately bonded enough yet to be giving it to her.

It took a few weeks for our little man to adjust to having someone else present, yet it was in this time of almost constant contact between the two kids that some spectacular healing took place. This young girl went from thinking she didn't want a younger sibling to becoming his absolute best friend. He has become her safe relationship. He loves her with no strings attached and no expectations. He loves her exactly where and how she is. When she walks in the door, he yells, "Si/Sissy!". She has become protective and caring of him, and she loves spending time with him. Watching them play together is one of the things that gives me the most joy that I have ever experienced because I know what it has taken to get there.

Letting her see the dynamic in our relationship with him was instrumental in her healing. She was able to witness what a healthy parent and child relationship looked like, and not just with her. She would observe and compare from her past my reactions and responses to both of them. She saw that I did not treat either of them differently. My reactions when he was upset or throwing a temper tantrum was one of calmness, gentleness, and love. I had this same response when I corrected her.

I hear you asking, "Well, what about your husband? Where was he in all this?" He was walking right beside me. She was able to witness what a healthy husband and wife relationship looked like.

She saw all the benefits that came from being with the right partner. Though things definitely weren't as easy for him and things took a little more time and effort, a relationship did form between them. Major breakthrough on this front began when we decided they needed bi-weekly father-daughter dates to help them grow and connect. She is his daughter through and through, and he is her Dad. I must say that I fell more in love with my husband as I watched him go through this process. I was grateful that something with the potential to tear apart other couples brought us closer together.

Over the summer we saw healing take place that is beyond words. The uncertain, self-conscious child started disappearing and was replaced by a beautiful, healthy and strong young woman. One day as we were standing in the kitchen she told me, "I was always told my whole life that I couldn't do things because I was handicapped. But now I know I can do those things and I'm not handicapped." This discovery brought a lot of emotions. She felt anger and grief over her past which she thought was normal until she met us. She also felt joy and excitement for the future. Her mind was opening up to the possibilities before her, and she was realizing she really could do anything she put her mind to. In fact, she made so much progress that we had new ADOS (Austim Diagnostic Observation Schedule) and IQ testing done in order to see where she fell on the spectrum and how best she learned. We wanted to set her up to meet the dreams she never before thought possible.

Even though she was fifteen, we were still able

to witness many firsts. These firsts included simple things like family dinners, game nights, riding the public school bus, and hanging out with peers and friends her own age. She began thinking about a future that involved moving away from home, going to college, and even having a job. The amount of healing and growth that took place in such a short time caused many to tell us that she was nothing short of a miracle! We have now reached a place as a family where people ask us how things are going, and we don't have a list of changes, accomplishments, or challenges to give. It is actually quite refreshing. We are simply us. When it comes down to it, everything feels like it has been this way forever. It is as if we have always had two kids with a huge age gap.

When we received our adoption date, it was a

few months later than we had been told. But, it would probably fall not only on my birthday, but also on the year-to-the-day that we emailed her team to set up a meeting about making her our daughter. This was the best birthday gift I could ever have been given! Beyond that, it was like our journey had come full circle; God was showing us that He really was in control. He sees the big picture.

When it comes down to it, I could sit and brag on both of my children and my husband for hours. They are amazingly wonderful and so perfect (even with their imperfections). Seeing them grow and bond and the healing and growth that accompanies that is beyond beautiful. I look back on my life and wonder if I would ever want anything different? Would I really change anything in this journey? All the trials and hardships led us to where we are now as a family. I feel like there is so much more I could put in this book, but it would be impossible to truly write it all.

In the midst of this journey, I went through my own process of healing and grief. I experienced a lot of things in my childhood that were not as they appeared from the outside. I was the bubbly girl that no one pictured getting mad at anyone. But I walked around with my own bitterness and anger accompanied by a deep sense of loss. It was on this journey that I was able to find healing.

People hear that we adopted a fifteen-year-old while in our thirties, and they seem to picture us with hands on our hips, wearing a tight, sexy costume including a cape flapping in the wind. I can tell you right now – we are not superheroes, and we are not perfect parents. We are no better than you. We do not try to be. We simply try to be the best version of ourselves. All children deserve this of their guardians. We should strive to be the best version of ourselves not only for them, but also for us. Does this mean we'll always be perfect and never make mistakes? Hardly. But as long as we move forward and try, they will see that effort and grow because of it.

People ask us if we plan to adopt again. The answer to that is yes. Absolutely. Then they ask if we are done having biological children. The answer to that is not as simple; I don't know that we can answer. I can hear some of you readers yelling in the back of your minds, "Tell them it's none of their business." You are absolutely right; it is not. But every time we are asked this question, I'm faced with my past. I'm faced with my brokenness. It's a past I want healing from, but it is also one that I have yet to receive with full closure. I just haven't been able to figure out where the closure lies. And that is okay. I've always wanted a big house brimming with children of all ages and races that feel safe enough to call us mom and dad. Every child deserves a safe, loving home with someone to believe in them. These are things healthy families take for granted. Thankfully, I have a wonderful husband who loves and supports me as I continue to seek healing. No, we don't see eye-to-eye in every situation, but we respect each other and desire only what is best for the other party.

As I draw to a close, I can tell you that foster care and adoption are not for everyone. Having children is not for everyone. Fertility treatments are not for everyone. Never feel like you need to compare yourself to others. Do what is right for yourself and your family. For those of you who have undergone any type of infertility, fertility treatments, or infant loss – remember that you are so strong. You fight a hidden battle of grief that no one else can see. For those of you who are foster and/or adoptive parents - I salute you. You are in a battle against the past for the hearts and minds of the kids in your household. Remember to practice self-care as you press forward. We have seen how the right environment can transform a child into who they are meant to be.

I do not write this make you think that I feel I am better than any of you or that my journey was harder. In fact, I know several people who I would openly say that their infertility, losses, and adoption stories are harder than my own. I write because my story can encourage others. I write because it was a door that opened up my healing. Each stroke of the keyboard allowed my soul to take flight and bring closure where it was needed and freedom where I felt trapped.

For those of you who read this and feel a tug one way or another for starting your own family - whether through natural means, fertility clinics, adoption, or fostering – know there are resources available for every situation. The best advice I can give you is to enjoy your journey, wherever it may lead.

44124619R00130

Made in the USA
Middletown, DE
03 May 2019